JOHN ELIOT'S
INDIAN
DIALOGUES

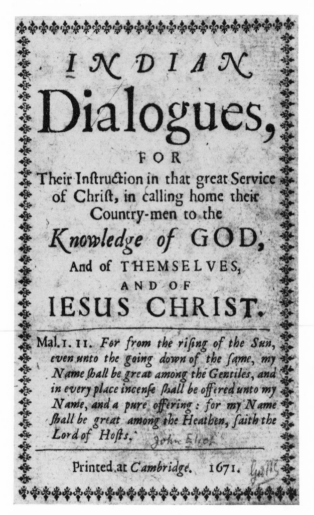

I N D I A N

Dialogues,

FOR

Their Instruction in that great Service
of Christ, in calling home their
Country-men to the

Knowledge of GOD,

And of THEMSELVES,

AND OF

IESUS CHRIST.

Mal. 1. 11. *For from the rising of the Sun,
even unto the going down of the same, my
Name shall be great among the Gentiles, and
in every place incense shall be offered unto my
Name, and a pure offering : for my Name
shall be great among the Heathen, saith the
Lord of Hosts.* John Eliot

Printed at *Cambridge*. 1671.

JOHN ELIOT'S INDIAN DIALOGUES

A Study in Cultural Interaction

Edited by
Henry W. Bowden and James P. Ronda

Contributions in American History, Number 88

GREENWOOD PRESS
Westport, Connecticut • London, England

Library of Congress Cataloging in Publication Data

Eliot, John, 1604-1690.
    John Eliot's Indian dialogues.

    (Contributions in American history; no. 88
ISSN 0084-9219)
    Dialogues which originally appeared in 1671, printed
by M. Johnson, Cambridge, Mass.; with introd. and
revisions.
    Bibliography: p.
    Includes index.
    1. Massachuset Indians—Missions. 2. Wampanoag
Indians—Missions. 3. Massachuset Indians—Religion
and mythology. 4. Wampanoag Indians—Religion and
mythology. 5. Indians of North America—Massachusetts—
Missions. 6. Indians of North America—Massachusetts—
Religion and mythology. 7. Eliot, John, 1604-1690.
I. Bowden, Henry Warner. II. Ronda, James P., 1943-
III. Title, IV. Title: Indian dialogues.
E99.M42E55 1981   266'.58744   80-542
ISBN 0-313-21031-4 lib. bdg.

Library of Congress Catalog Card Number: 80-542
ISBN: 0-313-21031-4
ISSN: 0084-9219

First published in 1980

Greenwood Press
A division of Congressional Information Service, Inc.
88 Post Road West, Westport, Connecticut 06881

Printed in the United States of America

10 9 8 7 6 5 4 3 2 1

Contents

Acknowledgments

Pascal said: "Some authors, speaking of their works, say: 'My book, my commentary, my history, etc.' They would be better to say: 'Our book, our commentary, our history.' " This edition of *Indian Dialogues* has indeed been a joint effort. We are grateful to each other for the patience and friendship that is demanded in any collaborative effort. Our thanks also to the staff of the Maag Library at Youngstown State University, most particularly Hildegard Schnuttgen, Helen Lesigonich, and Edgar Jones. We are especially anxious to acknowledge our debt to James Axtell, Neal Salisbury, William Simmons, and Jeanne Ronda for their steady encouragement during the long transcription and editorial process.

J.P.R.
H.W.B.

Introduction

Most seventeenth-century Europeans coming to the New World did not admit to finding anything admirable in the natives already here. English colonists who began occupying eastern Massachusetts in 1620 had been prompted by voluminous literature to regard local inhabitants as inferior. Direct observation increased their sense of cultural superiority to make the English disdain local Indian economy as wasteful, their habits as depraved, and their religion as idolatrous. By contrast, Englishmen presumed that their own cultural advantages justified domination of lands only recently known to transatlantic explorers. They sanctioned territorial encroachment with royal charters from home and sales agreements with natives who rarely understood the terms. But their major rationale was the pervasive conviction that no viable civilization existed in the occupied areas white men wished to take.

This attitude about land and its prior claimants shows that English colonists overlooked the solid weight of Indian customs and values. Their pervasive, fundamental assumption was that native Americans must either adopt European standards of living or suffer gradual attrition because there were no other practical alternatives. Peaceful co-existence, between separate cultures that respected the strengths and supplemented the weaknesses of each other, seems never to have been considered an option. This cultural myopia, characteristic of almost all expansionist white men at the time, blinded Europeans to the practicality, wisdom, and beauty of the red men's cultural systems.

Despite European prejudicial blindness, native American cultures were actually strong and numerous, evidence that intelligent human beings had learned to cope with their environment in a variety of sensible ways. In precontact times—before white men came to this continent—at a conservative estimate at least eleven million people lived in the vast territory north of the Rio Grande. They had formed no fewer than 250 separate cultural units of differing sizes, distinguishable by economy, dialects, social institutions, and political arrangements. Undergirding such multiplicity lay a number of unifying factors as well; geography and climate, linguistic stock, and shared culture patterns afforded some common denominators within the continental abundance of different lifestyles. Annual rainfall and soil chemistry, vegetation and animal life varied between the arid Southwest and the northern hardwood forests, but all tribes within a given ecological context faced the same challenge to creative adaptivity. Different peoples within a specific geographical area learned to share material items, which helped them cope with environmental conditions. Though some neighbors spoke different languages and claimed divergent lineages, they came eventually to share many religious and philosophical characteristics as well as material ones. This combination of geographical factors and human similarities in given areas allows us to speak of "culture areas": large collective categories that reduce most of the 250 native cultural units to a more manageable classification.

Culture areas such as the Southwest Desert, the Northwest Pacific Coast, the Great Plains, the Mid-American Prairies, or the Southeast Woodlands included a great number of native tribes. But the one which interests us at the moment was equal to these others in size and inclusiveness. The Northeast Woodlands constituted a large tract of land between the Atlantic coast and the Mississippi River, bounded by the upper Great Lakes and the Ohio River valley. In that large territory lived many different peoples with various languages and customs. But despite local preferences, woodland tribes of the Northeast shared conditions that shaped their economy, architecture, socio-political institutions, and religious ceremonialism along noticeably distinctive lines. Among the many tribes who lived in this congenial region, two of them merit our attention because they occupied the land where Puritans first landed. The Massachuset and Wampanoag tribes were both Algonkian-speaking peoples living in what is now southeastern New England, the former holding land around Boston Bay and the latter in a similar position around Narragansett Bay. They were also among the first native Americans to experience prolonged contact with English settlers; and before we inquire into missionary work among them, it is necessary to gain some understanding of their precolumbian way of life. Many generalizations about Massachusets and Wampanoags could also apply to other native peoples living farther west and south of them, but most of our anthropological description is derived from data about those two groups alone.

Estimated population figures for all of New England are tentative and sketchy, but many think it possible that over 100,000 natives inhabited the region before whites arrived. The Massachuset tribe with all its subgroups and affiliates consisted of approximately 22,000 people, while Wampanoag tribesmen also numbered about 22,000. These figures are based on estimates made in the very early 1600s. Debates about such statistics are largely academic, however, because whatever precontact tribal strength might have been, it was being drastically reduced through diseases introduced by the earliest European visitors. Between 1600 and 1620 fully half of all the humanity native to eastern Massachusetts and Rhode Island fell victim to fevers, pox, and other maladies to which they were not immune. The years of greatest suffering were 1617-1619 when an unknown infection swept the area and wreaked irreparable damage on the fundamental social matrix needed for holding local cultures together. By the end of that period, just when the Pilgrims started their small colony at Plymouth, local tribes had received a tremendous blow to the strength and leadership of their separate civilization. Thus reduced from their earlier vitality, the Massachusets and Wampanoags were not well prepared to sustain the initial period of intercultural contact.

Native Americans in this region had long prospered on a diet fairly evenly divided between agricultural items and the products of a hunting-gathering economy. Domesticated plants included corn (maize), several varieties of beans, squash, and pumpkins raised as food items, together with sunflowers (used for oil) and tobacco. While these plants provided the more routine staples of their food supply, Algonkians also depended heavily on meat acquired by hunting. Deer, bear, turkey, and many smaller animals taken in the chase supplied much of the fare. Shellfish, eels, and various types of fish taken by ingenious netting afforded other sources of protein. Berries, roots, nuts, and other wild seeds gathered in season also gave variety to a diet that was both substantial and well adapted to its natural setting.

Many commentators subsequently described New England tribes erroneously as nomadic huntsmen, totally dependent on the results of daily foraging through woods and coastal marshes. While it is true that the Massachusets and Wampanoags obtained a great deal of their livelihood from wild animals, early observers did them a serious injustice by implying that they were so dependent on hunting as to have no other resources for a balanced economy. Cultivated fields were an essential part of Algonkian subsistence, and their annual yield was conspicuous in supplementing the overall combination of foodstuffs that supported aboriginal life. Compared with other groups in North America who farmed extensively, such as the Iroquois in New York or the Pueblos in New Mexico, New England Algonkians did not rely heavily on planted crops. But they cultivated food supplies to a great extent, and it is wrong to think that they did not have the technical capability or practical judgment to grow staple crops as part of their reliable economic cycle.

Algonkian living patterns were intentionally diffuse and mobile, geared to fit their manner of coping with natural surroundings. Villages hardly ever remained at a single location for an entire year. If some did, dominating their area as strong palisaded locations, they hardly ever contained their full complement of residents through all seasons. Algonkian life was more given to regular movement within restricted geographical limits; it was neither truly nomadic nor rooted at perennial sites. A standard pattern would find perhaps thirty to fifty extended families living in mutual support of each other at one place. When spring came, they would plant crops in cleared fields and then move to the seashore or freshwater streams where fishing promised to be good. Then some or all of them would move to places where berries and nuts were known to grow in abundance. By autumn they would congregate at the first site again to harvest their fields and store food for the winter. In late fall groups or individuals would make prolonged hunting trips, and during winter small family units scattered to favorite hunting stations to make feeding easier. The cycle began again as the groups reunited in springtime for another round that started with planting.

Housing construction was admirably suited to this peripatetic way of life with its multiple residence system. The basic dwelling was a hemispherical lodge formed by a circle of poles tied at the top and covered with overlapping shingles or strips of bark. These *wigwams* were easy to build from local materials; they provided shelter from hostile elements, and their construction did not require time or energy out of proportion to their transitory usefulness. When it was time to move after a few months, old wigwams would be abandoned and new ones built at the next site chosen for the group's activities. Economy, village location, and architecture thus formed a coherent pattern in the Algonkian lifestyle. While there was little in it to convey a sense of essential permanence, still it possessed a diversified regularity that coped successfully with natural rhythms and sustained participants with a sense of accomplishment.

Kinship structure tended to include relationships beyond the pair-bond nuclear family, but many variations make it difficult to rely on any single descriptive word like "clan" to cover all types. Other group designations—technical categories such as sibs, gentes, and phratries—also existed in Algonkian kinship relations. The general point, though, is that extended families gave each member an enlarged sense of identity by belonging

to and sharing mutual responsibilities with a larger number of
people. These associations also functioned as an intermediary
between individuals and tribal ruling structures. They were a
source of psychological support in personal development, a
medium of expression in political activity, and a focal point of
loyalty in times of crisis. Among the Massachusets and Wampanoags such extended family groups tended to be patriarchal.
Not all Algonkian groups defined identity and inheritance
through the father, but quite often the basic lines of authority
in each wigwam, and in villages as a whole, followed patterns
dominated by male participation.

We do not know enough about various Indian cultures in
North America to say whether a strong reliance on hunting—
an activity monopolized by men—contributed to the preponder-
ance of male authority in kinship relations. We know little about
the extent to which Algonkian women supervised agricultural
activities, owned land, or participated to any substantial degree
in guiding family units. It could be that Massachuset and Wampanoag villages were evolving toward greater acceptance of female
contributions to family, clan, and tribal affairs. This may have
been the case, as male dominance seems to have diminished in
other tribes as their economies developed away from hunting
towards greater reliance on agriculture. Other cultures, more
heavily dependent on farming, showed a much more fully integrated use of women in native life. But this theory of cultural
evolution and economic determinism notwithstanding, all we
can say is that in 1620 most Algonkian tribes tended to be
patriarchal in defining lines of authority and patrilocal in
residence patterns. Basic elements of identity and inheritance
devolved patrilineally.

As with almost every other American Indian culture, once
clan identification was established for Massachuset and Wampanoag offspring, they were not allowed to marry anyone in that
kinship association. It was commonly held that such action was
incest, a crime that offended the *totem*, mythic grandfather of
all clan descendants. Marriages were almost always monogamous,
but there was little to prevent either partner from terminating
the relationship for any of a number of reasons. Divorce and re-

marriage were simple, prevalent features of tribal life that clan structures withstood without much damage to adults or children. Vocational training and role models survived the disruption of pair-bond relationships because clan members rather than biological parents provided them. Exogamous clans afforded the most important nexus for maintaining personal identity, and they facilitated cooperation in larger social issues where men did most of the deliberating on topics of current interest.

Larger structural units were organized under Algonkian headmen called *sachems*. While authority patterns differed throughout the Northeast Woodlands culture area, sachems generally tended to exercise control over social units made up of multiple clans. These men were not equals by virtue of office; their influence differed rather according to their diplomatic skill, personal charisma, and prowess in warfare. Sachems apparently maintained their office all year long and for life, unless some grave error discredited their status and caused the people to seek a new leader. Despite the fact that English chroniclers often used the word "king" to describe them, they did not approach that kind of extensive authority. Each Massachuset and Wampanoag sachem exerted influence over a segment of the tribe, but none controlled the entire population. Occasionally a strong sachem would extend his sway to cover many villages, and his words would receive special deference in great councils. But such power was the product of one person's individual attributes and competitive exertions, not laws about a traditional office. Each sachem's power fluctuated with changing circumstances. There was very little institutional structure to ensure loyalty towards a particular headman or even the concept of sachem, once alternative social patterns were introduced by whites. The subsequent social disintegration experienced by Algonkians after 1620 is at least partially attributable to their relatively simple, voluntaristic system of political leadership.

The main reason that Massachuset and Wampanoag political structures remained in such a "balkanized" state was because the people idealized personal initiative just as much as they did group conformity. Their social values were built on a foundation of corporate consciousness, but within that cohesive framework individuals were allowed great latitude to act on their own. Young men were encouraged at an early age to seek personal distinction through hunting skills, woodcraft abilities, and stoic endurance of physical hardships. When one excelled in games or other competitions, such honors came at the expense of other tribesmen; but competitive activities always occurred within the ego-sustaining camaraderie of local village geniality. In warfare great stress was laid on an individual's capacity to act bravely, to prove himself capable of leading fellow warriors in the forefront of an attack to vanquish enemies. Beyond his own village campfires each individual was encouraged to pursue additional honors in deliberating over tribal affairs or in representing his tribe in diplomatic missions to other territories. Much depended on the person's unique qualities of political astuteness, oratorical persuasiveness, and shrewdness in bargaining.

English accounts of Algonkian life frequently emphasize the disorganized character of village occupations in general and the "lazy" habits of men in particular. What observers failed to realize was the great respect for personal initiative that undergirded and encouraged this way of life. It seemed dissolute and badly organized to whites because most of them valued routinized lives and systematically industrious activity. They judged Massachuset and Wampanoag individuals to be indolent by comparison, but in fact the natives were simply free to choose their own objectives and to set their own pace for securing them. They could hunt or not, as their mood dictated. They were not required to participate in village councils or diplomatic missions. Activities in social and political spheres were open for all men to pursue as they wished, but it was entirely a matter of personal choice whether someone exerted himself or not. Once engaged in tasks such as hunting, trapping, canoe building or dozens of other pursuits, however, men accomplished their work with an energy and self-denying concentration that belied all thoughts of laziness.

Even warfare was voluntaristic. It is impossible to imagine anyone refusing to aid in the defense of his own village when attacked, but aggressive raiding parties were another matter.

They comprised only those who voluntarily agreed to support the venture. No one was obliged to join a raiding party if he chose not to, and no social opprobrium applied to those who remained at home. Leaders of aggressive forays announced their intention of conducting war on some enemy target; other warriors responded positively or negatively as their feelings suited the occasion. Young men almost always accepted invitations to participate because they sought opportunities to acquire prestige and gain the higher social standing that came with military glory. Others, young and old, could remain indifferent to the project and decline it without dishonor. No sachem or field general could forcibly assemble Algonkian warriors for any given campaign because native respect for individualistic behavior overruled thoughts of coercive recruiting. The usual pattern of local warfare was a series of small scale attacks and retaliations wherein individuals strove to display personal valor. Whenever an exception occurred to this voluntaristic custom, as in 1675 when the great majority of Wampanoags fought as a single strike force, the effect on English settlements was devastating.

Individualistic action characterized most areas of human experience in Algonkian societies, while communal values supported each person's right to decide on the extent and quality of his participation. Of course techniques such as persuasion, ridicule, and example-setting acted as controls to ensure a degree of village conformity, but the predominant trait in Algonkian behavior was its atomistic tendency. Individuals were understood to be on their own, seeking excellence in personally chosen areas where their unique skills could be put to best advantage. There were hardly any social organizations to enforce or enhance these pursuits, no corporate structure to confer extra power or to train them in additional capabilities. Just as Massachuset and Wampanoag individuals were free to express themselves in areas of their own choosing, they were similarly alone when it was necessary to face tensions and traumas in life. This was especially so after white men increased the pace of cultural interaction. There were few structural supports for confronting Puritan society because of this basic esteem for

individualistic initiative among New England Indians. In the
confusion and disorientation thus experienced in subsequent
cultural conflict, Algonkians had little to rely on other than
their varying degrees of personal determination to resist the
influence of white technology, customs, and ideas.

Another aboriginal value providing a significant contrast
with that of white colonists had to do with land and attitudes
about owning it. For the Massachusets and Wampanoags, as
with almost every other native American group, land was considered a basic part of the nurturing environment, part of the
universally shared created order that everyone held in common.
It was not a commodity to be parcelled out in sections or controlled by individuals without reference to other members of
their cultural unit. For all the initiative granted to other types
of personal behavior among Algonkian-speaking peoples, the
idea of a single individual's using a plot of land for his exclusive
benefit never occurred to them. Of course each tribe and every
subgroup had a sense of identity with and sovereignty over the
land that formed the perimeters of their existence. But the idea
of someone's claiming irrevocable title to the land, distinct
from tribal use, was as absurd to them as trying to own the air
or sunlight. Sachems could assign areas for temporary use by
specific groups; they could not transfer land to an individual
for ownership in fee simple or for selling it again in a private
transaction.

It would be wrong to think that Indians were selfish about
land ownership or that initially they were reluctant to share
territory with whites. When colonists first arrived, Wampanoags
and then Massachusets met the newcomers in a manner con-
sistent with their code of hospitality. They charitably allowed
whites the use of fields for planting and choice locations for
houses. But when they discovered that Puritans wanted to keep
those tracts exclusively for themselves, without title ever revert-
ing to the group originally granting privileges of using it, bitter
resentment inevitably followed. Indians were unable to compre-
hend the European pattern of land ownership because none of
their experience corresponded to anything like it. They considered land to be part of their sacred universe, an aspect of the

divine order of things, held in trust for posterity. For someone
to have the selfish audacity to insist on restricting part of the
soil for his exclusive control was beyond their comprehension.

Indian folkways were often regulated by ceremonies and ritualized behavior that gave significance and a sense of propriety
to every routine. The primary focus of leadership in those religious
activities was the shaman, usually called *powwow* in New England.
Powwows flourished in almost every village, and they served in
varied ways including dream interpretation, curing, predicting
the future, and acting as intermediaries between human and
spiritual levels of the integrated cosmos. Natives believed
shamans were capable of entering trances wherein their souls
left the mundane sphere to commune with spirit beings. Once
they revived or became whole again, they relayed special mes-
sages from divine powers to designated individuals or to the
entire group.

Powwows guided religious activities in Algonkian tribes by
functioning as seers, prophets, and spokesmen for the groups'
collective awareness of the supernatural. In addition to articu-
lating this cognitive aspect of religion, they were commonly
respected for an ability to change their body shape, to assume
animal forms, and to accomplish secret tasks undetected. Natives
believed they had power to cause illness by "shooting" alien
objects into people's bodies. They possessed as well the corres-
ponding ability to diagnose what an enemy powwow had done
through similar devices. Maladies that today we might call psy-
chosomatic could be cured by the local powwow when he extracted pieces of shell, stone, hair, bone, or feather that were
thought to have struck down a victim. The Massachusets and
Wampanoags along with other Algonkians believed in witch-
craft, but there was no generic difference between that and the
power exercised by a powwow. The distinction was simply a
matter of perspective. A powwow in one camp was deemed
useful to his group if he could inflict damage on opponents
by weakening rivals with illness or killing them outright. That
same individual was feared as a witch by enemy camps because
of the same activities. Positive or negative reactions to a powwow's influence differed according to how one experienced it,

but the power was essentially the same and occasioned great
deference in Algonkian circles.

Powwows were the only significant religious figures in Massachuset and Wampanoag villages, but their influence was limited.
To begin with, success depended on individual performance.
Those who filled shamanistic needs faced constant pragmatic
testing; continued recognition of their status depended on successful completion of the services that local inhabitants asked them
to provide. Every powwow was left to his own resources to
meet those entreaties. There was no priestly brotherhood to
bestow religious powers through ordination, nor did a society
of powwows exist to support individual practitioners in their
spiritual efforts. While some powwows in New England followed
common preparatory rituals such as fasting, sweat lodges, and
sexual abstinence, none of them felt compelled to accept any
uniform set of liturgical rules. Personal innovation and judicious
choices earmarked each seer's ritual behavior, and eventual success depended on ingenuity, not inherited formulas. Powwows,
as individualistic religious functionaries, reflected in their sphere
of action the pervasive Algonkian idealization of personal
initiative.

Another important restriction of powwows' authority lay
in the fact that local inhabitants could either support them
or transfer their allegiance to some other visionary. Just as an
adept's shamanistic abilities were effective only as long as he
actively exhibited them, so his influence survived only as long
as he could persuade tribesmen to acknowledge it. Socio-
political leadership among the Massachusets and Wampanoags
was held by sachems, and that office remained fairly constant
in New England. Religious leadership embodied in powwows
found less support in an institutionalized power base because
many individuals could exhibit shamanistic feats at various
times and thus acquire personal followers. Their sphere of influence expanded or contracted according to the practical benefits they could provide, and once-powerful powwows could
sink into obscurity if popular acclaim shifted to new individuals
who displayed greater success in performing spiritual tasks.

A third factor suggesting the precarious nature of shamanistic eminence in Algonkian societies is the fact that their religious powers differed from that of common people only in a matter of degree. There was nothing that set them apart from other tribesmen except a facility for accomplishing what everyone else could do, at least at certain times in their lives. Powwows were gifted tribesmen, different from fellow villagers only because of a proclivity for visions, trances, and prophecy. Native Americans prized the intrinsic value of such experiences and freely consulted those who manifested a better-than-average capacity for communing with spirits. But such consultations were voluntary, and people required tangible, beneficial results for continued support. There was no institutional foundation for the office of powwow other than a general opportunity for individuals to display their spiritualistic abilities. Community support depended on results, and when Puritan influence began assaulting various aspects of native life, that support wavered. Especially when missionaries directly challenged local spiritual leaders, there were few institutional lines of religious authority to sustain those who wished to resist white culture and rely on the traditional role of powwows.

Every person in Massachuset and Wampanoag culture was relatively free to vary from loose norms regarding dress codes, civic responsibility, and military participation. They were also allowed wide latitude regarding forms of religious expression. Indians recognized many different means through which divine-human encounters could be experienced. Emergency situations often required tribesmen to consult a powwow; yet at other times they tried to accomplish the same results with a less mediated approach. Powwows were usually consulted during times of sickness or when collective village interests came into consideration. But many other occasions called for private visions, direct communication between the seeker and those guardian spirits who chose to reveal themselves for his personal benefit. Especially at the age of puberty, youths were expected to establish vision contact with the supernatural world. They tried prolonged fasting, isolation in sweat lodges or in wilderness

seclusion, sexual abstinence, and watchfulness without sleep
as standard means of inducing the experience. Such mild physical sacrifices and supplicatory prayers often resulted in a dream-
like state wherein the individual saw divine beings and communicated with them on a personal level. Those instances of
supernatural contact confirmed the Algonkians' general sense
of living close to many spiritual powers. Such encounters also
determined quite specifically the direction, content, and tone
of each participant's subsequent lifestyle.

Divine beings usually appeared to humans in the form of
animals or some other transfigured phenomenon. Visions could
recur, and new visions could be obtained by those who were
sufficiently steadfast in their questing. Such experiences sanctioned local folkways as each generation participated in them,
while at the same time spiritual freedom opened the way to
constant modification of ritual activities. Visions were the core
of social conservatism, and yet they were also the source of
important new departures from custom. In the Massachuset
and Wampanoag view of priorities, it mattered less whether
people acted to preserve or alter patterns than whether they
based the actions consistently on the validating experience of
genuine visions. Dreams had a place in directing personal action
too. Unanticipated experiences of clairvoyance were also
recognized as important in providing goals and a sense of
proper orientation. But prolonged visions, for which individuals
prepared deliberately and carefully, were the essential feature
of privatized religion among Algonkians.

Spirit beings who appeared in naturalistic forms to individuals
did so because they chose to favor those seeking visions. Whether
they appeared only once in a lifetime or communicated with
the questor periodically depended on their inscrutable will.
Seekers of visions could usually affect their private gods through
sincerety and persistence, but in other areas there were more
formalized rituals for dealing with divine powers. Hunting was
an especially important sphere, in which Algonkians took pains
to treat spirit beings with respectful, ceremonious acts of propriety. Animal spirits were thought to be easily offended by
menstruating women, for instance, and females in that condi-

tion were rigorously kept away from hunters. Men successful
in a hunt often performed simple rituals over the fallen animal,
apologizing for having taken its life and wishing its soul well as
it journeyed back to the spirit world. Failure to act in such a
manner could anger all animal spirits and bring famine by
causing game to leave the region. Disrespect shown to an animal's
bones could also offend spirits. Algonkian hunters were particularly careful not to mistreat the bones of a bear, neither burning
them nor letting dogs eat them. In that way they hoped to preserve the good will of spiritual powers who provided a great
portion of their subsistence.

This variegated, complex pattern of ritualized behavior among
hunters is the best example of a basic characteristic that appears
countless times in native American religions. The Massachusets
and Wampanoags treated salient aspects of their environment
with a reverence born of knowledge that animals and plants,
mountains and rivers, indeed all phenomena possessed supernatural qualities of their own. Just as cordial relations between
humans called for expressions of courtesy and mutual deference, it was equally necessary to show proper respect for other
forms of life. Much of Indian religion consisted of ritualized
behavior that expressed such an attitude. In that manner
Algonkians hoped to maintain a correct set of relationships
with other inhabitants of the cosmos, securing their cooperation and blessing through ceremonies thought to be pleasing
to the various personalities.

Whether someone asked for safe passage on a journey, tried
to placate a menacing spirit at some dangerous locality, invoked
aid and protection prior to battle, apologized to the bear-spirit
after killing one of those animals, petitioned the favor of earth
spirits at planting time, or made any of a hundred other prayers
regarding the outcome of life's experiences, Indians recognized
that many different powers surrounded their own level of existence. Conduct related to home life, food gathering, community solidarity, and dealings with enemies—all these involved
ritual duties as well as the performance of menial tasks. Rituals
were taken seriously as basic components of what constituted
effective action. Natives who ignored ritual duties were bound

to fail in life because they disregarded the larger context of
reality and risked offending a great number of ubiquitous personalities. Those who employed correct rituals faced their environment confidently, knowing that their ceremonious acts
acknowledged the deference and cooperative respect demanded
by the controlling powers.

Native American identification with group, place, and appropriate ritual found confirmation in their overall view of reality
that made daily attitudes meaningful and appropriate. Rituals
provide us with a better source for understanding Algonkian
religion than mythology does because Indian myths are quite
diffuse and vary often in names and details. Either Massachuset and Wampanoag worshipers did not give high priority
to narrative explanations, stressing immediate awareness of
divine powers instead, or white men have long since obliterated
the old mythological records. All we can say now is that there
is no evidence of a single normative creation story that shaped
native religious consciousness, no general account of the origins
of the cosmos, environment, animal, and plant life, or humanity.
Different Algonkian stories abound, but they do not constitute
a unified sacred text that dominated the mind and controlled
the activities of those who used them. While such tales offered
a variety of explanations about origins and meaning in the
world, none was taken as authoritative. Stories were not sys-
tematized, and multiple answers to a single question were cheer-
fully tolerated as equally satisfying accounts of universal themes.
Activities described in mythic narratives suggested many norms
for behavior, but there was no resultant uniformity. No one
concluded that all Algonkians should act the same way any
more than they were supposed to think alike. Although myths
supplied a loose rationale for Algonkian religion, they afforded
little specific, binding content. They were used in ways that
permitted room for intellection, but the native Americans who
used such myths laid greater stress on concrete personal religious
encounters.

Surviving mythological narratives show that they sustained a
religious consciousness recognizing divine qualities in all different forms of life. The most striking Algonkian term for godly

power was *Manitou,* but it is impossible to say whether natives used that word for an exalted monotheistic deity in precontact times. After whites arrived, it seems that Manitou came to resemble Jehovah as a local counterbalance to Christianity. But before those changes Manitou was generally associated with heaven, sky, or the sun, often with all powerful rhythms of life, a concept conveyed by translating the divine name as "Great Spirit" or "Master of Breath." More important for actual religious practice is the fact that Massachuset and Wampanoag peoples believed in countless lesser beings, *manitowuk,* who inhabited local surroundings and directed the course of daily affairs. Without distinguishing between natural objects and the spiritual presence in them, Algonkians treated all aspects of their world as living personalities. Plants and animals, stars and stones, mountains and rivers, clouds and lakes—all these phenomena were thought to be alive, imbued with intelligence and supernatural force. These had to be taken into account throughout the course of human activities. Divine power existed everywhere, and encounters with spirits had to be expected at every turn of events. New England Indians placed no strong reliance on one god with multiple capacities, nor did they develop a clearly defined hierarchy of deities who controlled different spheres of life. Each daily activity and objective had its own sacred aspect. For Algonkians this fragmented but homogenous view of the world was more realistic than more inclusive or generalized theories. The ubiquitous, localized presence of thousands of manitowuk was agreeably attuned to popular religious behavior that stressed individualistic responses to spirit beings directly involved with each person's experience.

Among the many other reference names characterizing Algonkian myths, one more common denominator bears mentioning. Stories did not often indicate creators, protectors, or malicious personalities, but many of them centered on the paradigmatic actions of a culture hero. Such tales usually depicted facets of the culture hero's life to explain how the present world came to be the way it is: why rivers flow downhill for example, why corn is a particularly important plant, or how fire originated. Names for this culture hero differed from one tribe to another;

but a favorite referent was *Wetucks* (var. *Moshup*), who was believed to have existed since early times, when local inhabitants needed help in learning how to master their environment. Wetucks set about aiding his people by fashioning conditions for their corporate benefit and by teaching them the skills necessary for successful ecological adaptation. Such a culture hero seems not to have been worshiped as a god, though his activities clearly exhibited superhuman knowledge and ability. His chief function in tribal lore was to legitimate present conditions, explaining them in terms of narrative antecedents conformable to both a dawn-time precedent and a contemporary psychological mind set.

Wetucks was often accompanied by an enigmatic alter ego, sometimes a twin brother, who produced the opposite kind of results. Whether through spite or more frequently through a sense of prankish mischief (occasionally because of sheer bungling), the work of this trickster figure accounted for the less pleasant features of life. Many good things in human existence were due to Wetucks; failures, hardships, and death were attributable to his opposite number. In some Algonkian groups a single mythological figure, sometimes termed "Great Hare" or "Rabbit Man," combined both positive and negative qualities in inchoate action that accounted for varied conditions as they were currently experienced. But regardless of whether these polarities were attributed to two individuals or to contrary impulses in one figure, the Indian worldview posited no sharp dichotomy between good and evil. Life was acknowledged to be mixed with joy and pain, triumph and suffering, with no particular design embodied in various combinations. Good and evil were just different aspects of a single framework where positive and negative forces operated with indifferent fatalism, only sporadically altered because of human supplications. Algonkian views of the world maintained an integrated tension among the several elements of such a cosmos. They avoided dualism but did so without resolving confusion about ultimate meaning or helping to choose between various moral options.

In rough outline these were the primary components of the Algonkian mythological thought that gave cognitive structure to a native view of the world. Together with corporate rituals and a fundamental emphasis on personalized communication with spirits, these supernatural referents helped give meaning and orientation to everyday activities. Massachuset and Wampanoag tribesmen were generally satisfied with life as they understood it. When death inevitably occurred, they were confident that the same basic features of present-day existence would continue beyond the grave. As with most other native American groups, they did not stipulate a place of punishment for the wicked and another of reward for virtuous citizens. They looked forward to residing in a place where everyone would be reunited after death, inhabiting the same type of villages and pursuing the same kind of lifestyle as before. Their way of living and general view of reality were compatible enough to reinforce each other, affirming the patterns that local residents used to cope with environmental challenges. They accepted such conditions as essentially supportive, and they pursued a life of adaptive cooperation as the proper approach. Death posed no ultimate threat because it did not terminate the exuberance of living. In another realm beyond temporal problems, Indian existence was expected to triumph over the grave and to open new horizons where individualistic accomplishments would again flourish with undiminished vigor.

II

By the early 1600s many left-wing English Reformers decided that emigration was the only effective means of escaping religious corruption in their homeland. Both the Separatist Pilgrims who settled Plymouth Colony in 1620 and non-Separatist Puritans of Massachusetts Bay Colony in 1630 came to the New World hoping to build model communities of godly living. Another principal end of their colonizing effort, stated quite early in the course of events, was to win natives to a knowl-

edge and obedience of the Christian faith. Thus missionary
work among native Americans was declared to be one of the
central justifications for establishing towns on the seacoast and
expanding into the interior. But efforts toward that end lan-
guished for more than a dozen years in New England; practical
considerations of survival seem to have preempted any altruistic
sharing of the gospel message. Initially English statesmen and
clergy spent most of their time shaping a temporal and ecclesiastical form of government to exhibit the best form of Christian
civilization. Their priorities centered on achieving righteousness
for themselves and building new plantations, not on converting
those who already occupied the territory.

The earliest sustained missionary effort was inaugurated by
Thomas Mayhew, Jr., among Algonkian-speaking Indians who
lived on Martha's Vineyard. After the elder Thomas Mayhew
acquired proprietary rights to the whole island, young Thomas
began in 1642 to converse with natives in their own language
about religious matters. Because of his patient efforts, and the
fact that few other whites were around to interfere with his
progress, some notable conversions had been achieved by 1657.
In that year, however, New England's first missionary was lost
at sea when the ship on which he was traveling to Europe dis-
appeared. Thomas Mayhew, Sr., continued the work begun by
his son on the land that he monopolized as something of a
feudal domain. His grandson followed suit, and, all told, five
generations of the Mayhew line gave Christian guidance to the
natives of Martha's Vineyard and Nantucket for the better part
of two centuries. Though there may have been more than a
hint of patriarchal condescension in their work, it stood as an
early example of steady evangelical enterprise, producing some
undoubtedly beneficial results among people who responded
to gospel exhortations.

Several other New England ministers became interested in
missionary work during the seventeenth century, but their
efforts did not convince most of their fellow clergymen that
native Americans needed the gospel. During almost one hundred
years no more than twenty Congregationalist ministers tried
to reach local tribesmen, and none of them concentrated ex-

clusively on missions. Only a handful produced noticeable results, and considering the proportion of converts to total native
population, none of their work can be termed outstanding. If
we judge from nothing more than declared intentions, it seems
that Englishmen were just as committed to Christianizing
American Indians as were the Spaniards and Frenchmen who
occupied other parts of the continent. But English colonists
actually produced the smallest number of missionary personnel,
allocated less financial support for their work, and exhibited
greater indifference toward missions than other Europeans. In
spite of the fact that some Puritans acquired deserved fame as
Indian evangelists, their special concern about native souls was
ignored by most white men around them. Missionary work in
early New England disclosed a lamentable gap between rhetori-
cal manifesto and actual implementation.

Reasons for this neglect of a primary motivation go much
deeper than a general sense of cultural superiority and disdain
for native American customs. All whites, Spanish and French,
Dutch and Portuguese, as well as English, looked down on
Indians because European technology produced better tools
than native artisans could make. But it was the English who
seemed most disdainful of this fact and least concerned to
preserve any aspect of native civilization. Most Englishmen did
not care to preserve the aboriginal peoples, even if they could
be persuaded to adopt the values, habits, and materials of the
colonists' superior culture.

One factor that accounts for some part of the New Englanders'
scornful attitude about Indian cultures has to do with their
prior experience in Ireland. Since Elizabethan times Englishmen
had been accustomed to viewing the truculent Irish—a separate
culture and religion that they were trying to dominate—as barbarous pagans who would not accept the manifest advantages
of British influence. In America that preconception transferred
easily to Indians, who indicated a similar reluctance to acknowledge the superiority of English life. Then too, these Englishmen
were Puritans. Because they had left Old England because of an
unwillingness to compromise on matters of belief and conduct,
they were not about to look favorably on deviant customs in

a setting under their control. Puritans were religiously and culturally aggressive, against all forms of behavior they considered
ungodly. They were as intent on converting the lives of whites
in Boston as they were on changing the customs of Massachuset
warriors. This zeal had caused them to colonize a new territory,
and they were deeply concerned to establish a haven for those
holding their own confessional viewpoint. As a persecuted
minority fleeing to this continent from episcopal interference,
they gave priority to maintaining security for their own "tribe"
instead of expanding their influence at once to include others
of an alien civilization.

Such cultural factors might help explain why Englishmen
were not generally disposed to accept Indians as equals, but it
does not show why so few clergy tried to convert natives or
bring them "up" to white cultural standards. One cannot accur-
ately say that Calvinism contributed much to their religious exclusivism or overweening posture of cultural superiority. Puritans genuinely believed in the arbitrary nature of God's inscrutable will, granting saving grace to some individuals while
withholding it from others. They affirmed that salvation
depended on divine foreordination and not on human attempts
to affect God's predetermined decrees through acts of pretended
virtue. This conviction was the sobering prerequisite to a type
of thinking that kept believers humble before a sovereign deity
who moved in mysterious ways to accomplish His purposes.
The predestinarian aspect of Puritan theology often produced
a sense of self-assurance among those who felt chosen by God's
grace, but such spiritual elitism did not apply to all members
of any nation, socio-economic class, or racial group. As Calvin-
ists were willing to admit that the Almighty could touch a
Massachuset soul with the experience of saving grace as easily
as He had apparently redeemed a select number of Cambridge
graduates, there was little theological justification to account
for their inattention to missionary responsibility.

An additional factor pertinent to the lack of missionary zeal
among Congregationalists had to do with their distinctive conception of ministerial status. If someone studied theology,
learned to preach acceptably, and passed the scrutiny of exam-

ining pastors on points of doctrine, he could be ordained a
minister of the Christian gospel. But that individual was recognized as a clergyman by legal designation and community acceptance only as long as he served in a ministerial capacity. If he
terminated that vocational responsibility for any reason other
than moving to a different church, he was no longer considered
a clergyman. The number of ministers in Puritan colonies thus
corresponded to the number of churches, the total growing in
tandem with increased population and territorial settlement.
But there could be no surplus of ministers, nor were there re-
tired persons still claiming the social status of clergymen. A
minister was defined through association with a specific church.
Without it, he joined the ranks of pious laymen who contributed
to the general pattern of religious activities that was ancillary
to their central vocation. Congregationalist ministers knew that
their clerical standing was tied directly to providing satisfactory
service for their local parishioners. In those days it was not
thought proper for someone to be ordained as a minister and
preach only to Indians without a white parish to legitimate his
existence. Whenever missionaries devoted any time at all to
neighboring tribesmen, it happened only when they could afford
time away from their primary duties as pastors of white churches.

These brief considerations help account somewhat for the
relative paucity of seventeenth-century English missions to
native Americans. But after such factors are given full weight,
the fact remains that the English as a whole did not treat
Indians as persons having a value or respectability of their own.
Puritan missionaries differed only slightly from this general
cultural arrogance. They saw the unregeneracy of red and white
civilizations alike as sinful, deserving of censure yet eligible for
salvation. Missionaries agreed that Indians were depraved and
uncivilized in their natural state, but they also thought natives
could respond to grace and change their habits, qualifying as
members of new covenanted communities. Still, their efforts
toward enlarging the Kingdom of God with native converts
were minimal and secondary to other activities. Compared with
Spanish and French missionaries in similar situations, Puritan
clergymen were never as energetic or self-sacrificing. Spanish

Franciscans or French Jesuits, often among the first explorers
to establish contact with various native peoples, lived close to
local tribes for evangelical purposes. Puritan ministers, on the
other hand, never lived among their native charges during the
seventeenth century, and their contact with Indians occurred
long after other Englishmen had determined the general pattern
of cultural exchange. By the time ministers began preaching the
gospel to Massachuset and Wampanoag tribesmen, great inroads
had already been made on native cultures by explorers, soldiers,
land speculators, traders, and farmers. Instead of being on the
leading edge of red-white cultural exchange, English missionaries
trailed behind almost every other aspect of the social process.
Whether through preference or circumstance, Puritan evangelical
work seems generally to have been an afterthought, not a primary
motivation, in the enterprise of colonizing the New World.

In that enterprise, though, a few ministers did attend to
Indian missions. Over the decades notables such as Richard
Bourne on Cape Cod and John Cotton, Jr., at Plymouth added
their names to the short list. Samuel Treat preached to Indians
around Eastham, while Grindall Rawson of Mendon and Samuel
Danforth of Taunton dedicated their spare hours to the effort
as well. But of all those who worked to evangelize the natives,
none matched the reputation of John Eliot, pastor at Roxbury.
Eliot was born sometime in the late summer of 1604 in Wid-
ford, England. His childhood training seems not to have been
rigorously pious, since he attended Jesus College, Cambridge,
instead of that university's strongly Puritan Emmanuel College.
Receiving his bachelor's degree in 1622, Eliot apparently took
orders in the Church of England. We know nothing about his
life for the next seven years, but in 1629 he became assistant
at a small school run by Thomas Hooker, later one of the
founders of Connecticut. Eliot's associations show that by then
his religious views had definitely gravitated toward Puritanism.

Conditions in Archbishop William Laud's England convinced
many would-be reformers that they would have to conform to
increased restrictions in the national church or accept exile
from their homeland. In 1631 Eliot decided to join others who
sought freedom in the New World to achieve their ideal of

Christian excellence. Sailing aboard the *Lyon*, he landed at
Boston in November and served for a time as teacher in the
church there. Members asked him to remain their associate
pastor, but in 1632 Eliot honored what seems to have been a
prior agreement and became minister at Roxbury, a post which
he held for more than fifty-seven years. He also taught school
to augment his salary, providing secular education as well as
religious nurture for two generations of townspeople. During
the Pequot War (1636-37) Eliot became aware of Indians in his
region for the first time, and it may be that his interest in converting them began that early. But he did nothing about it for
another six years. Then in 1643 he began learning to speak
Algonkian, and three years later he was able to preach elementary
sermons in the local dialect.

Over the course of time Eliot endeavored to place Algonkian
among the literate languages. He compiled a dictionary and
grammar, furnishing as much a guideline for his own learning
as for natives whom he taught to read. In 1654 he printed an
Algonkian translation of the Shorter Catechism and seven years
later published the New Testament for Massachuset converts
to read in their own tongue. Finally in 1663 the complete Bible
appeared, *Mamusee Wunneetapanatamwe Up-Biblum God.*
Eliot persevered in literary attempts to edify tribesmen, translating Richard Baxter's *A Call to the Unconverted* (1664) and
Lewis Bayly's *Practice of Piety* (1665) in addition to issuing
several shorter religious tracts. In native settlements where he
had any influence, the schoolmaster was as prominent as the
minister, and in 1669 his helpful *Indian Primer* appeared as a
means of starting young minds on the road to intellectual as
well as spiritual enrichment. Most of Eliot's other writing was
in English, advertising among British readers the success of
mission work and aiding the solicitation of funds. In 1649
Parliament created what is most often called the "New England
Company" and authorized it to collect money for Indian missions. Eliot began receiving a stipend shortly thereafter, and
over subsequent decades several ministers acquired supplemental
income through that agency which lasted for more than a century.

In 1646 Eliot began preaching in Natick dialect, at first halt-

ingly but then with increasing ease through the next forty years.
His initial attempt in September was little short of disaster.
Addressing some Massachusets who lived near Dorchester under
a sachem named Cutchamekin, he tried to explain simple biblical truths. But instead of responding to the point of his message,
the natives asked him to explain the cause of thunder, the
source of winds, and how tides operated with such regularity.
Daunted by this failure to communicate his ideas effectively,
Eliot withdrew to his study for more preparation. Then on
October 28, 1646, he met with greater success. He spoke then
to a small gathering of men, women, and children assembled at
the wigwam of Waban, a petty headman who lived at Nonantum
near Newton. For more than an hour he preached about the sinfulness of all mankind, reminding his listeners of the dreadful
wrath God stored up for those who broke His commandments.
After dwelling at length on Christ's sacrifice and the coming
judgment, he ended by describing the blessed estate of those
whose Christian faith yielded joy in heaven and depicting just
as vividly the horrors of hell in store for wicked unbelievers.

Natives did not of course immediately accept ideas so un-
familiar to them, but Eliot's preaching at least started the
process whereby some Indians eventually embodied as genuine
a set of Christian beliefs and conduct as their white co-religionists. During those first contacts Eliot and his fellow missionaries
hardly noticed compatible elements that would have allowed
Puritans to meet local natives on common religious ground.
Aboriginal cultures as well as Calvinist commonwealths were
deeply conscious that spiritual forces presided directly over all
features of human existence. Algonkian tribesmen readily acknowledged that the world was not of their own making. This
quality of general religiosity was expressed in such various ways
that it is impossible to speak of a uniform native creed or
standard liturgy. But the major point is that a fundamental religious sensitivity already directed the thought and behavior of
New England Indians before Christians began missions among
them. The native concept of Manitou was analogous to Jehovah.
Both deities were usually identified with the sky or heavens,
at least to the point of distinguishing them from spirits of the

forest and subterranean regions. This common recognition of a
"god above" should not be pressed too far, however. Manitou
was an impersonal deity, while Jehovah was elaborately anthro-
pomorphic as well as an abstract power. Still, such terms indicate that compatible ideas existed that could have served as
avenues of mutually profitable religious discussion.

Another area of general agreement lay in the widespread
affirmation among native Americans and Puritans that everyday experience was constantly affected by the supernatural.
Whether blessings or hardships came their way, individuals in
both religions attributed their daily lot to the wills of divine
powers who directed events according to higher purposes.
Indians called them manitowuk, while the English referred to
angels as agents of supreme Jehovah. But a common pattern
held in both cultures, in that people were urged to cooperate
harmoniously with immortals who influenced their lives. Each
group interpreted good harvests, successful hunts, and military
triumphs to be the result of their collaboration with spiritual
forces. They saw personal misfortune, natural catastrophes,
and national defeats as punishment for human wrongdoing.
In this general framework where supernatural power dominated
mundane affairs, both aborigines and Puritans invoked the aid
of higher beings. Private prayers as well as communal ceremonies were thought to be effective means of approaching the seats
of divinity. So when Eliot and other missionaries preached to
native tribesmen, they already shared a fundamental respect
for supernatural influence over temporal affairs, and both appreciated the importance of ritualized deference to godly beings.

There were also many contrasting elements in the two religious
orientations. Puritans were strict monotheists, and they condemned worship of lesser objects as idolatry, something that
compromised adoration of the one true God of the universe.
Drawing upon a stern prophetic tradition, they denounced multiple holy figures because such an array confused and detracted
from single-minded devotion. They criticized Roman Catholics
for venerating saints, but native Americans made even worse
religious mistakes. Puritans thought it was unalterably wrong
to deify natural phenomena or to imbue physical objects with

a spiritual life of their own. Whether native thought was based
on actual polytheism or simply recognized various localizations
of diffuse supernatural power, Indian spiritualism contrasted
sharply with the Puritans' monotheistic exclusivism. Another
antithetic point lay in the fact that Puritan ideas derived from
a specific biblical tradition while Algonkian religion was rather
flexible in ideological content. Christian leaders tried to deter-
mine proper conduct according to a normative theological
standard that they considered valid for all circumstances.
Indians defined their behavioral guidelines more pragmatically,
considering group interests and individual needs as varying conditions presented them with fresh problems needing expedient
solution.

In keeping with their grimly predestinarian version of Reformed thought, Puritans also emphasized the depravity of
human nature and the need of divine grace for regeneration.
Indians did not perceive human life as congenitally wicked in
its constitutive elements or in deliberate attempts to behave
well. Of course natives distinguished between good and evil
according to their own standards, but they did not see human
failings as symptoms of a perverse appetite. It never occurred
to them to threaten death and damnation for those who trans-
gressed community expectations. Puritans viewed natural man
as totally incapable of living up to God's righteous demands;
Indians considered everyone capable of interacting harmoniously
with the divine powers who regulated their universe. New
England Congregationalists put a premium on deliverance
from humanity's endemic corruption. Local tribesmen found
it hard to appreciate salvation because they saw no need of being rescued from an essentially positive state of existence, so
full of practicable ways to enjoy it.

It was difficult enough for Indians to understand Puritan con-
victions about sinful humanity, but the intricacies of how divine
grace operated to redeem sinners pointed up even greater contrasts between the two religious perspectives. After trying to
digest the unsettling news that they were indeed depraved and
without hope except for heavenly forgiveness, natives were
probably more disconcerted to hear that they could do nothing

at all to influence God's decision about their fate. Still, if they felt stirrings of unmerited grace within them, missionaries insisted that they should respond in specific ways to obey the Savior's will. Efforts to lead a sanctified life stemmed not from attempts to aid the salvation process or to cooperate with benign spirit helpers; Christian propriety sprang from a sense of joyful duty which only the chosen few were privileged to realize. All those lacking the experience of grace were doomed to everlasting punishment, a fate which their inherited proclivities and misdirected actions richly deserved.

The Massachusets and Wampanoags had never conceived of a hell for tribesmen whose misdeeds called for retribution. They thought sacrilegious acts would prompt negative reaction from the gods almost immediately, just as socially destructive behavior met swift communal reprisal. But they assumed all natives would eventually reside together in the same place after death. Christianity threatened to destroy that aboriginal understanding of community. It menaced tribal solidarity by declaring that only individuals could be saved. The new faith separated them from all the rest who did not share its privileged status. This palpable exclusivism was a logical extension of Puritan doctrine. Its disruption of corporate identity stemmed from the fundamental belief that Indians, like all human beings, were permanently separated into the elect and non-elect, destined by God never to see each other again after this lifetime.

In noting differences, it is important to see that these two religions utilized strikingly dissimilar types of leadership. Puritanism received its specific content from professional specialists who drew churchly standards from biblical tradition, perceived through their own culturally conditioned viewpoint, of course. New England clergymen were highly trained, and they seriously tried to meet their responsibility of monitoring every citizen's deportment. Their work focused on exhorting church members to greater approximations of Christian perfection, but it extended also to advising magistrates on most civil affairs. Religious activity among Massachusets had much less uniform structure and authoritarian guidance to it. Indian pow-

wows rarely took the initiative in guiding communal behavior.
They provided religious leadership when consulted about
specific problems, but they did not occupy a place of sufficient
spiritual eminence to provide stability and cohesion to natives
challenged by missionaries. Puritan ministers could demand a
modicum of respectable conduct from everyone within their
sphere of influence, but Algonkian religious spokesmen allowed
wide latitude to individualistic worship and morality deemed
appropriate by various practitioners. The two religions differed
significantly, not only in their views of human nature and ultimate destiny; they also relied upon contrasting kinds of leaders
who affected daily conduct along differing institutional lines.

In actual practice Puritans made little use of the compatibilities
shown to exist between native religions and their own. They did
not emphasize common ideas or show how Indians might use
them as bridges to move from indigenous patterns to Christianity. Missionaries chose rather to heighten the contrast between
Indian religiosity and their own by denouncing all precontact
ideas and rituals as abominations. With few exceptions, English
references to Indian practices censured them as "barbarous,"
"heathen" and "uncivilized." Puritans shared the Englishman's
general sense of cultural superiority over native ways, but they
added moral indignation to that prejudice and held a self-
righteously negative attitude about aboriginal patterns. Missionaries looked at local tribesmen and saw only laziness, thievery,
drunkenness, blood lust, nakedness, sexual promiscuity, and a
congeries of religious superstitions. The handful of Congregationalist ministers who visited native villages may have been
moved by compassion for the depravity found rampant there;
but their message was primarily one of condemnation, a warn-
ing of God's wrath and a promise of eternal torment for those
who continually flaunted the Almighty's law of righteousness
as found in Scripture.

Implausibly, this denunciatory stance which Eliot and other
New England missionaries adopted did produce a few Massachuset converts over the years. According to reports meant for
British consumption, some native Americans acknowledged
themselves to be sinners and showed signs of genuine repentance,

all of it evidence to Puritans of divine grace. Preachers thought
their persistent gospel efforts shed enough light to call it the
daybreak if not sunrise of Christian hopes for New World inhabitants. While we cannot ignore the possibility that Indians really
understood Puritan theology and were sincere in confessing the
operation of grace in their souls, other factors played a part as
well. Early missions yielded few positive results in places where
native cultures were still relatively intact (like the Wampanoag)
and strong enough to resist. But after the fiber of precontact
culture had been weakened by disease, loss of land and manpower, and increased dependence on European trade, conversions increased considerably. Many who seemed to choose a
new way of life over old preferences were actually indicating
the impossibility of maintaining their traditional lifestyle under
English domination, politically, economically, and now religiously. Missionaries contacted Indians later than many other participants in the overall sequence of red-white interaction. They
did not instigate native decline and never self-consciously based
their evangelism on a policy of eradicating all precontact customs. But despite whatever altruism they possessed, missionaries in New England depended upon, and probably accelerated,
the pace of cultural disintegration among native residents.

Even in conditions of political fragmentation and cultural
disorientation, not all villagers adopted the white man's religious
perspective. They accepted new material goods rather easily,
but the deep psychological roots of religious loyalty were less
susceptible of change. When conversions did occur as an aspect
of selective borrowing, they often seemed part of the syncre-
tistic framework already prevalent among New England Indians.
Some of them were willing to add the white man's deity to
their pantheon, just as they were assimilating kettles, hatchets,
fishhooks, and blankets into established subsistence patterns.
Others adopted Christianity under crisis conditions, for example,
when a general sickness swept Martha's Vineyard in 1646.
Since fewer Christian Indians appeared to be sick than scoffers,
many natives concluded that the monotheistic faith had better
protective power than they originally had noticed. After that
some converts regarded baptism as preventive medicine. Others

came from the ranks of once-influential sachems and powwows who accepted new rubrics to retain some of their old standing. In 1651 Cutchamekin, Eliot's early opponent, accepted ruler-ship in a Christian Indian town primarily to keep a modicum of his diminishing eminence. Such factors as these, secular and religious, operated during the complex processes termed "con-versions." Whatever motives came into play, some aboriginal peoples did respond favorably to Puritan preaching, and they emerged as a distinctive entity known as Praying Indians.

Given the Puritans' strong emphasis on doctrine—with con-current stress on cerebral activities such as sermons, study classes, and reading—many converts showed remarkable sophis-tication in adapting to new religious norms. Missionaries in-sisted that understanding must precede confession and that rational assent prepare the way for ritual participation. One exception to this rather thoroughgoing religious imperialism is the fact that Eliot and others used native language instead of English in communicating their evangelical program. That single concession to precontact patterns allowed Christian Indians to preserve some of their old identity while they changed in most other categories. Under Puritan tutelage many learned to treat religious propositions with the gravity of systematic theologians. The importance of such behavior is not that they could make what some whites considered rudimentary steps toward theological comprehension. Its real significance lies in the fact that they were willing to accept a new conception of religion, one that gave almost exclusive priority to cognition. Puritans made little use of pictoral art, dance, rituals, dreams, or individualistic communion with spirit beings. Algonkians had been accustomed to utilizing all those forms before conver-sion, and it is a measure of their inner change to see that they virtually abandoned such practices, conforming to the English-men's narrow version of what true religion ought to be.

In preaching the Word of God, Puritan missionaries thought they served as avenues through which divine grace could touch the souls of those predestined to live among the saints. Some natives responded positively to those exhortations, and that confirmed the whole Calvinistic order of things. Unlike Catholic evangelists who relied on the efficacy of sacraments in their missionary efforts, Puritans insisted that baptism did not convey saving grace to the recipient. Indian converts in New England were baptized as a sign of grace already experienced inside them. The ritual only symbolized an internal regeneration wrought by divine agency; it did little to enhance any native's spiritual condition or improve the quality of daily conduct. Those who accepted the new view of cosmic order—with its omnipotent triune deity and His injunction to join the true circle of worshipers—were then urged by missionaries to develop the subsequent marks of Christian behavior. As an alternative to sacramental helps, nonliterate natives were taught to read in their own language. Once that crucial plateau had been reached, Praying Indians were encouraged to read edifying tracts, books, and above all the Bible. That was the means of acquiring practical guidelines for spiritual improvement.

These cognitive aspects of a Reformed orientation constituted the marrow of Puritan divinity, and native converts accommodated to it with a fair degree of competence. On the tangible level, though, missionaries required Praying Indians to adopt an equally thoroughgoing set of changes. They took great pains to clarify specific behavior that was expected of Christian believers. Much has been written about how Puritans wished to destroy native customs and let their superior ethical standards fill the resultant vacuum. But broadly speaking, this is a commonplace observation, because practitioners of most religions tend to equate their faith with dominant ideas and accepted behavioral norms of their day. Puritans did not differ in this self-assurance from European Catholics or from most native American groups within their distinctive cultural orientations. This is the context in which we can understand what Eliot meant when he said that Indians had to be civilized before their conversion was complete. He was neither unique nor devious to think that natives should repudiate their indigenous culture and rise above former shortcomings by adopting an essentially English way of life. Still, such Puritan ideology led to complicity in the destruction of native cultures and their wholesale replacement with British patterns.

The key to understanding the cultural impact of Puritan missions is a theological one, an emphasis on sanctified living that
had to follow regeneration as part of the salvation process.
Once a person experienced justification through faith, he received additional grace to achieve righteousness in all outward
aspects. Puritans insisted that godly living had to follow as a
tangible sign of the inner miracle already begun through God's
regenerative forgiveness. Mere conformity to the high moral
standards of genuine Christians could not save anyone, but
Puritans strongly rejected the antinomian suggestion that redemption experience released everyone from a strict code of
Christian conduct. Ministers exhorted all believers to moral
probity, seeking improvement among the whole population
too because colonists did not measure up to the biblical requirements of a righteous nation. Puritan action among native
converts stemmed from the same theological drive that also admonished whites to mend their faulty habits and to foster virtue
with divine help. Missionaries did not want to destroy Indian
cultural standards simply because they were Indian; they did
so because they thought them wrong and displeasing to God.
They sought to transform the customs of all who fell short of
biblical precepts, and this zeal for cultural surgery applied to
Stuart courtiers, Anglican prelates, and common yeomen as
well as to natives of the New World. Of course, when Puritans
gave specific content and direction to their ideal of sanctification, they like others drew ethical principles from historically
conditioned mores. In teaching Indians how to live a full
Christian life, they were actually teaching them to act like
Englishmen. In pursuing such an evangelical program missionaries helped destroy native cultures, but they did not direct
converts' lives in new directions for economic benefit or for
their colony's political advantage. Eliot and his confreres were
basically religious agents who sought to enhance the salvation
of souls and a gradual achievement of Christian perfection. In
retrospect we can see that they mixed their own customs with
biblical teachings to an uncritically comfortable degree. All the
while they thought such standards transcended limitations of
time and culture. But they were wrong, and that is one of the

ironies of missionary history. Conversion to Puritanism implied
a change in belief and behavior in everyone accepting their
yoke of salvation, but the number of changes required by their
brand of Christianity actually transformed the lives of Indians
more than it did other targets of Puritan evangelism.

One of the major changes in store for Praying Indians was
settlement at a permanent townsite. That situation created an
environment conducive to all the other modifications missionaries wanted to make among their converts. Beginning with his
early sermons to Waban, Eliot urged natives to accept the related links of Puritan religion: trust in God's unmerited forgiveness and obey His will through communal discipline. By
1650 he persuaded followers to end their semi-nomadic subsistence patterns and to locate for all seasons at Natick. Over
the next quarter-century he was instrumental in establishing
fourteen such towns. In addition to Natick the principal ones
were Punkapaog, Hassanamasitt, Okommakamesit, Wamesitt,
Nashobah, and Magunkaquog, all located an average of twenty-
five miles from Boston. Perhaps settled towns made it more
convenient for preachers on periodic mission tours to find
listeners; they certainly made it easier for natives to seek practical Christian improvement without the distracting influence of
unconverted tribesmen. It is impossible to say whether Eliot
placed converts in new towns to make them politically sub-
servient to the Massachusetts Bay government. But whatever
the reasons, his enthusiasm for nurturing Indian Christianity at
permanent locations set the stage for a wide ranging alteration
of precontact behavior.

Whereas Massachuset tribesmen had customarily relied heavily
on hunting and gathering to feed themselves, settlement in
towns made such an economy virtually impossible. They were
still able to hunt occasionally—Natick comprised 6,000 acres,
Punkapaog had 8,000—but confinement inevitably pointed to
intensive agriculture as a new economic base. In addition to
planting larger gardens, Praying Indians developed orchards
and began raising cattle to supplement their diet, becoming
incipient capitalists in the bargain because they sold the surplus.
Instead of living in wigwams, many at Natick learned enough

carpentry to build solid houses of English design. They laid
out three streets and constructed a combination meetinghouse
and school too. In a strictly physical sense Praying Indians accepted many changes in daily conduct. They became familiar
with mattocks, spades, crowbars, and hammers. Persons were
urged to cut their hair, wash off the bear grease that protected
their skin, wear European clothes, and dwell as nuclear families
in separate houses. Contrasting perhaps most strikingly with
traditional practice, they also built fences to enclose plots of
land for private use.

Social values changed along with physical arrangements as
native converts tried to conform to the Puritan ideal of proper
conduct. Formerly the clan had provided a secure matrix in
which tribesmen received identity and found outlets for personal
initiative. Once individuals began accepting Christianity with
its new way of life, attitudes about clans and other tribal institutions were severely modified. New loyalties, especially to the
church as an alternate identity-giving structure, replaced the
old reliance on kinship relations. Larger family associations did
not often transfer intact to Praying Indian towns, falling victim
to the new insistence on permanent monogamy sanctioned by
Christian ceremony. Natick and other towns contained converts
from many bands, and the familiar basis of native political
authority rarely survived transition to the new scheme of things.
The visiting minister and local exhorters or elders were the real
leaders now; they superseded traditional political figures by
virtue of their seniority in the new faith. Of course powwows
were hardly welcome at all, but if one converted and asked ad-
mission to a native church, he renounced all former powers as
an unpleasant reminder of a degenerate past.

Native life in New England had valued many forms of personal initiative in warfare, councils, vision quests, and displays
of valor. Puritan strictures about private and group action placed
severe limitations on individualism in Praying Indian towns.
Eliot set a precedent at Natick by supplying rules for what he
hoped would become a model Christian community. Basing its
constitution on what he saw as a biblical prototype (Exodus

18:25), he drew up rules to promote virtue and discourage vice. Indians adopted those requirements in order to embody the sanctified life which all genuine converts longed to achieve. The old style of personal freedom gave way to new standards of piety that everyone in the township was expected, often forced through fines or flogging, to follow. Many Massachusets also radically altered their former psychological attachment to the land. As they often broke ties with clan and tribe to accept the new faith, they usually felt closer to fellow confessors who had moved to Christian towns as a result of similar experiences. Church congregations replaced native adherence to kinship structure, and Praying Indian townships gave converts a new sense of locality to replace their earlier regional consciousness.

The practices of Indian Christians did not often resemble their earlier mode of living. Converts changed a great deal and tried over the years to repudiate vestiges of former habits. Except for retaining their original language, Massachuset converts seem to have permitted a rather thoroughgoing metamorphosis of their lives. In attempting to explain their susceptibility to change, we must recognize that they had never had strong social institutions to give precontact traditions much of a resistant framework, particularly in the area of institutionalized religious leadership. When intercultural tensions increased because of pressure applied by missionaries, Algonkian individuals could rely on few corporate organizational forms to sustain them in customary beliefs. Individuals had to deal with those tensions by themselves, and some decided to accept the white man's beliefs as well as his trade items. To be sure, sachems and pow-wows resisted such change because it eroded their status. But because their prestige was based on voluntary acceptance, they could not prevent individual decisions to accept a new way of life, though it seemed subversive to the old. Once converts began adopting English usages, there was little to check a gathering momentum toward almost total acceptance of new patterns.

Another factor explaining change among Indian converts is the fervent zeal behind Congregationalist ideology. Puritans were a religious group still battling to establish their position

on the Christian map, and they resolved to make their part of
the world over again according to rigorous standards. This
grim reformist determination stemmed from a need to succeed
as well as from the omnipotent deity who was supposedly its
ultimate source. The combination of weak aboriginal institutions and vigorous pressure from Puritan missionaries as well
as magistrates makes the cultural collapse among converts more
easily understandable. Compared with other native American
groups who used precontact structures to resist European missionary efforts, New England Indians possessed relatively
limited means of preserving cultural integrity. This is nowhere
better exemplified than in Praying Indians who accepted a
thoroughly changed worldview and ethos by conforming to
English notions of proper human existence. For some their
transformation was complete, and they became red Puritans.

It would be wrong, though, to think that all members of the
Massachuset nation accepted Christianity, lived in model towns,
or subjected themselves to the virtues enforced there. Natick
comprised no more than thirty families in its early days,
counting about 145 persons willing to inquire further into
Christianity. In 1674, the high point of mission success, only
1,100 natives lived in all of Eliot's fourteen special towns.
Missionaries in Plymouth Colony reported a total of some 500
converts in their area; Martha's Vineyard and Nantucket claimed
up to 600 families. Those figures represented hardly 10 percent
of the native population on the mainland, and even then most
of those residing at missionary sites were considered only
potential Christians, as yet unbaptized. Eliot's missions could
count only 119 baptized natives, with a mere seventy-four of
them in full communion with covenanted churches. There were
fifty at Natick, sixteen at Hassanamasitt, and eight at Magunkaquog. Statistics alone are not an adequate measure of successful
missions, but they help us appreciate the circumstances in which
Eliot worked. They show, however, that by the early 1670s his
missions did not include massive numbers of converts, nor had
they changed the basic lifestyle of most natives. This was the
context in which he wrote *Indian Dialogues*, in hope of extend-
ing the mission and rescuing more souls in the New World.

III

The dialogues reprinted in this volume are rare. They first appeared in 1671, printed by Marmaduke Johnson, late "Cittizen and Stationer of London," then residing in Cambridge, Massachusetts. Though many segments of Eliot's writing have been reproduced in later histories and anthologies, no portion of the *Dialogues* has reappeared during the past three hundred years. Only two known copies of Eliot's original publication have survived to the present time, a circumstance that in itself is a strong reason for making it available again. One copy resides in Oxford's Bodleian Library, while the other is kept in the Lenox Collection at the New York Public Library. Modern students of early New England have had access to these documents through microfiche cards in the assembled Early American Imprints, but now it is possible to reproduce those seventeenth-century pages in convenient book form to enrich general knowledge about both the ethnography and the religion of that period.

In the preface to his work Eliot admits that the dialogues are not historical chronicles of discussions between missionaries and nonbelieving Indians. His writing presents instead a series of imagined encounters between Praying Indians and other natives. But the fact that they are not factual records does not make the dialogues valueless. They were based on Eliot's own trial-and-error experience with Indians and can be taken as a distilled paraphrase of important issues that recurred frequently during his long ministry. So while not constituting stenographic reports, they still serve indirectly as historical documentation. Deriving as they do from Eliot's interaction with local tribesmen, they also furnish anthropological data that corroborate our understanding of native attitudes and ideas. Finally, they stand as an interesting contribution to the venerable tradition of apologetic writing. Since approximately A.D. 90, when Justin Martyr composed *Dialogue with Trypho*, Christian authors have used dialogues as a literary vehicle to explain, defend, and recommend their point of view. Eliot's work fits that genre, conveying the basic tone of New World evangelical labors to those unacquainted with them and defend-

ing the truth of Puritan beliefs for those confronting native
religions.

We know that Eliot wanted to use his dialogues as a training
manual for native missionaries, and that also helps us use the
material as historical documentation. In a letter to Richard
Baxter dated 27 June 1671, he wrote about his efforts to instruct
Christian Indians in various branches of useful knowledge. Then,
closer to his interest, he raised the "great point of church work,
to send out either officers, or brethren, to call in kindred and
countrymen unto Christ, as we are in the actual practice of it."
In native churches Puritan missionaries relied on a considerable
number of local residents for continuity and religious leadership. Instead of subordinating Indians to continual dependence
on white clergymen, Eliot encouraged natives to accept ministerial responsibilities. By 1671 every large Praying Indian town
had at least one lay exhorter; several had preachers. For a time
it seemed that Indian churches would thrive with an ethnically
compatible leadership able to keep pace with increased mem-
bership. And to that end of increasing the number of believers,
Eliot reported to Baxter, "so I have drawn up a few instructive
dialogues which are also partly historical." By having Christian
Indians read his dialogues he could rehearse chosen emissaries
in dialectical reasoning. He could anticipate objections likely
to be made in actual discussions and show his trainees how to
prevail over expected difficulties.

So as a historical document the *Dialogues* gives us valuable
information about John Eliot and his time. It reveals the priorities of his own evangelical work among Massachuset villages
while preserving at least some of the central religious attitudes
of converts who responded to his preaching. The work also reflects Eliot's concern to portray his charges as orthodox believers to the larger Christian world. Perhaps this is why the
book was originally printed in English rather than Algonkian.
As an exercise book for native missionaries, an Algonkian
version would have been more helpful, but unforeseen difficulties prevented any intended translation. An additional benefit
expected from this publication was to make a favorable impression on the Commissioners of the United Colonies. Eliot hoped

to show civil magistrates that Praying Indians were sound Christians, steadfast in correct doctrine, and obedient to lawful authority in civil as well as ecclesiastical offices. That is why he petitions the commissioners early in the book, asking them to defend converts because of their deserving character. If colonial authorities protected Indian land and water rights from avaricious whites, then Eliot believed that confessing townships would flourish and their churches have a bright future "in after ages." Such a mixture of motives behind the book, intended for red and white audiences in different settings, make the *Dialogues* worth considering in our time as a window on the past.

The first dialogue begins with a proclamation of the gospel incorporating native idioms. But that announcement does not mince words in emphasizing the contrast between two styles of living. Eliot discloses a typically Puritan attitude about pre-contact life when he has a native missionary describe it as "filth and folly." He regards village dances and games to be "noise" at best, "works of darkness" on a more sinister level. The whole panoply of Indian life merges with that of "wolves, bears and other wild beasts" to reflect a common English assumption about the wilderness they faced. It is interesting that Eliot portrays Christian Indians as having adopted this apprehension regarding primeval desolation too. More telling contrasts are based, though, on the fulcrum of religious insight: Christian truth versus pagan falsehood, of which all behavior is merely extension. So Indian missionaries leave no doubt from the beginning; they have come to root out a depraved way of life and replace it with correct beliefs that nourish true piety.

Native reactions to this abrupt announcement disclose their old loyalties. They ask if God is a superior powwow, if He can protect followers from sickness and poverty while providing them with material blessings. The missionary tries to point beyond mundane preoccupations to spiritual concerns, but non-Christians in the dialogue return again and again to the practical expectations they customarily placed on religious relationships. In response to further demand for tangible benefits, the native Christian recommends some of the spiritual attractions so dear to converts. But not many listeners find the "narrow

heavenly ways" so manifestly attractive. After listing the major
differences again, the missionary concludes, "Your joys are
bodily, fleshly, such as dogs have, and will all turn to flames in
hell to torment you." Some unbelievers challenge the source of
those ideas as well as their summary judgment. They suggest
that Englishmen have concocted the whole story as a means of
subduing Indians through fear of imaginary punishment. Eliot's
deliberate inclusion of such an objection shows that Indians
probably made the accusation often, and he took pains to refute
it. But the evangelist's reassurance on that score is not convincing, and villagers persist in saying, "We are well as we are, and
desire not to be troubled with these new wise sayings."

At that point in the dialogue there is a subtle shift that slow-
ly produces increasingly favorable responses from listeners.
The missionary ends his abrasive comparison between religions
and begins demonstrating his piety through practical examples.
His explanation of personal ritual propriety is something natives
can more easily understand because native religion had always
stressed meaningful ritual over theological propositions. But
many remain distant; becoming Christian seems so difficult,
and if there is no advantage to converting, it would be folly to
abandon tested ways. Seizing that argument, then, the missionary points out that God truly does benefit human life. He provides food, especially the venerable corn plant, together with
water and game animals to sustain life. At that point Eliot
depicts natives (rather unrealistically) as warming to the
Christian message. But the important thing to notice is that
villagers begin to listen more respectfully after they understand
how the new religion applies to their present lives in a practical,
day-to-day fashion.

Shifting to another scene, a sachem and a powwow are given
opportunity to voice their objections to the missionary's intru-
sion. As guardian of traditional folkways, the sachem complains
that potential converts would have to give up too much to
accept the new faith. He too prizes conventional wisdom and
asks why missionaries claim to be wiser than the legendary
keepers of tribal lore. The powwow repeats the view that pre-
Christian customs are satisfactory and that native gods are suffi-

cient, especially as their large number can obviously accomplish more than any single deity could. All the prayers, sacrifices, and healing rituals of precontact religion seem beneficial enough to preclude change. But the missionary responds to all these defenses by contrasting God's omnipotence with the false gods and sinful life of non-Christian culture. Apprehension and contrition seem to be mounting in some listeners; so the powwow falls back on Algonkian individualism and defends religious diversity, saying, "Let us alone, that we may be quiet in the ways which we like and love, as we let you alone in your changes and new ways."

Still, the contrived dialogue is meant to anticipate conversion, and thus its final scenes convey a sense of genuine religious interest among villagers who have heard the missionary. One of them demonstrates the strong corporate-mindedness indigenous to Indial social values, even while contemplating change. In the face of accepting Christianity, which isolates individuals for salvation, he says, "I am loath to divide myself from my friends and kindred. If I should change my course and not they, then I must leave and forsake their company. . . . I love my sachem, and all the rest of my good friends. If I should change my life and way, I greatly desire that we might agree to do it together." Eliot was astute enough to recognize this strong native attachment to community identification, and he tried to preserve it minimally by urging group conversions or by transplanting believers to Christian villages. The dialogue ends with an extended explanation of Sabbath observance, one of the most important features of Praying Indian towns. Practical demonstration of ritual and personal example again prove more effective than airy debate. And though both sachem and powwow find enough reasons to put off accepting Christianity, others seem more receptive. Those almost persuaded fear their inability to read and worship correctly, but the missionary promises to send another adviser to tutor the souls touched by God's Spirit.

The second dialogue seems to be a companion piece to the first. Whereas earlier conversations gave ample room for natives to state objections to gospel pronouncements, this dialogue is transparently a vehicle for orthodox Calvinist doctrine. The import of discussions here is that Indians have the same spiritual experiences as white converts do and that God works among all men with an awesome consistency familiar to the elect. It also shows that Puritans took native thought patterns seriously only so far as to wean converts away from them. Once they progressed to the real crux of spiritual introspection, the psychological profile and theological terms employed fit completely within the Puritan frame of reference. An ancillary motive behind this dialogue might have been to defend Indian Christianity by displaying its solid grounding in Calvinist theology. If white skeptics wondered whether native converts were sound in Christian priorities, the speaker in this second dialogue displays a biblical dexterity and soteriological reasoning power that would settle all doubts.

Doctrines explained in this discussion are a miniature catechism. The native chosen to delineate such beliefs is Waban, headman at Eliot's first successful preaching station and subsequently officer at Natick. His explication of God as creator and lawgiver, of man as sinner fated to die, of the Trinity, the person and work of Christ, ending with general observations about human repentance, is impeccably and succinctly Puritan. Also in line with that kind of reasoning, he does not suggest that persons might turn to God from their own motivations. His peroration on regeneration ends by affirming the lack of free will: "who wrought this great change in you? It was not your self did it, nor was it I that did it. I only opened unto you the word of God, but the spirit of God, by the conviction of the law, and by the word of God, hath wrought this work in you. . . . [T]he spirit of God by the word is able to create faith in you to believe in Jesus Christ." Similarly, embryonic Christians are able to perceive the true workings of divine grace in their souls, even as it is happening.

Following regeneration, the convert avers that nothing less than full Christian sanctification will do for him. Waban outlines the distinguishing marks of a practicing Christian, and it is worth noting that he does not mention here anything antithetical to indigenous customs. Indians could remain ethnically

distinct and add prayerful habits to their lifestyle. Still, conversion involved a degree of reform because the second element
of sanctification required diligence against backsliding. Pious
Christians are also expected to read the Bible, to use the catechism as key to the Scriptures, to study at home and train
their children, to observe the Sabbath at public gatherings, and
finally to maintain exemplary conversation while doing good
to others. This is a rather stylized and truncated version of
Puritan advice on applying Christian precepts to life, but it
shows that Eliot's pastoral concern lay in disciplined pieties
rather than political or economic behavior.

The second section of dialogue II recapitulates earlier doctrines, spoken this time to one who says, "I am old and cold
and dry, and half dead already. I have not strength enough left.
to be whetted up to such a new edge." But Waban insists that
the gospel applies to lives almost spent as well as to young ones
full of promise. He preaches a singularly inappropriate sermon,
biblically accurate but full of metaphors such as vineyards,
grapes, and wine which had no native counterpart to aid their
understanding. Still the call for repentance comes through at
the end, despite cultural differences separating preacher and
listeners. This time the final note is severe, almost desperate,
instead of pleasantly expectant. There is a sharp word of warn-
ing and a call for submission before death puts repentance out
of reach. Invitation and threat were never far apart in the
Puritan's urgent attempt to rescue souls from perdition.

In dialogue III we turn again to questions of cultural impact.
The person representing traditional viewpoints this time is
Philip, a Wampanoag headman whose bloody rebellion a few
years later traumatized red-white relations. But five years before that fateful episode, Eliot depicts Philip as having serious
thoughts about Christianity. We know that Eliot and his son
actually visited Philip's village several times in years previous
to issuing these dialogues, but it is unlikely Philip ever expressed
as much interest in the new religion as he is here made to do.
Perhaps Eliot hoped that the Wampanoag chieftain might
eventually develop a positive regard for Christian precepts.
Perhaps he thought it would do no harm for readers of his book

to think that Philip was so inclined. At any rate the historical
Philip differed significantly from the fictional one presented
here, and this is where Eliot strains poetic license to a painful
degree. Still, the missionary begins by appealing to Philip's civic
responsibility, not by denouncing unenlightened barbarities.
With the discussion placed on that footing, it is not too difficult to believe that the real Philip could have said, "I begin to
have some good likance of the way, but I am loth to buy it at
so dear a rate."

The brunt of Philip's response is a detailed recounting of that
cost. His first two arguments against the new faith are that conversion would destroy him politically. If people accept Christianity, they will reject him as their sachem, he argues. Or, if
he becomes a Christian without his fellow tribesmen, then he
loses social influence by abandoning his constituency. The
missionary assures him on the first point that true worship is
not inimical to civil office. Philip should feel no threat because,
though Christian citizens require political leaders of their own
faith, the Bible enjoins them to obey lawful authority in secular
affairs. Evangelical answers to the second problem seem less
convincing. Saying what Philip did not want to hear, the missionary explains that conversion often involves giving up lesser
goods to attain God's blessing. In terms that strike us as particularly unconvincing to a political leader, the preacher argues
that Christian sachems are better off without unbelieving followers because they were the worst sort of men anyhow. How
much better to grasp everlasting life instead of fleeting power
in worldly concerns. But with some consideration for the
sachem's mundane interests, he reminds Philip that accepting
Christianity would place him in better standing with colonial
magistrates and royal authority, while simultaneously pleasing
God.

Another pair of objections against a sachem's converting
pertains to his public image. If a headman enters the new faith,
he would lower himself to equality with his townspeople and
thus jeopardize his social standing. Missionary response to this
point is a cold rebuff. The preacher reminds Philip that Christianity is indeed a leveler among men because God is no re-

specter of persons. This must have struck the proud chieftain the same way it has threatened aristocracies around the world in all ages, but the missionary is firm. In religion sachems enjoy no privileged status, although salvation does not threaten their political role. Indeed, church order establishes and supports civil order, while God defends it too. Similarly Philip argues that church discipline will deteriorate his rule because it subordinates him to common citizens. While this is true, the missionary urges him to see that discipline is good for his soul and that admonitions delivered in church are made tenderly without intending to shame the offender. It is worth noting in this regard that few sachems or powwows in New England actually became Christians.

A final pair of demurrers remind us of questions raised in the first dialogue. Is the Bible really God's word or just an English trick to conquer us, and if this religion is so good for us, why did our forefathers not embrace it, transmitting salvation through our own tradition? Attempting to settle such doubts, the missionary appeals to internal evidence in the Bible to defend its veracity. Then beyond that tautology he quotes the catechism and tries to vindicate Scripture by recounting its marvelous contents as well as the author who inspired it. This elaborate discourse on biblical authenticity leaves little room for answering the question about why previous generations of Indians were ignorant of Christianity. Presumably, once natives realized they possessed such riches as the Bible held, they would abandon traditional loyalties without hesitation.

Within this latter discussion Eliot introduces a strong anti-Catholic diatribe. His point is to show that the gospel conflicts with traditional wisdom in many cultures, some of them even claiming Christian ancestry. By unmasking the deliberate malpractices of Catholic rulers and churchmen, he allows Philip to observe, "They are worse than our powwows. . . . I see that in some places of the world there be worse men than we Indians be." So in addition to making for good reading back in Britain, Eliot's antipapal pejorative tried to show Indians that reliance on any human tradition fell short of God's righteous demands. The discussion with Philip culminates in calls for repentance

and promises of pardon. Its final note is a vigorous defense of
Sabbath observance, which always held a special attraction
for Eliot.

After expounding his favorite ideas on Sabbath holiness,
Eliot shifts the scene to an imaginary future time. Philip is no
longer mentioned by name, and we can only speculate if the
Wampanoag leader is projected here as a penitent Christian
inquirer. In fact this literary setting creates a fourth dialogue.
Its theological concerns resemble those of dialogue II and give
symmetry to the total work. In dialogue I Massachuset persona
discuss the cultural impact of Christianity with missionaries
who lead them through misapprehensions to positive response,
which is then nurtured (dialogue II) by a more purely theological interchange. Now Wampanoag spokesmen go through a
similar intellectual transformation depicted again in twin conversations, both of them comprised within segments of dialogue III.

but more than mere knowledge

Puritans were close observers of psychological experience in
conversions. Many of their pastoral writings counseled inquirers
and believers at various stages of spiritual progress. In this
attenuated dialogue we begin with entreaties from a disillusioned
sachem who wishes to discern God's will in all the wordly cares
that distress him. As Puritan spokesmen are really in their element here, the Indian missionary uses all his companion's tur-
moil to claim that God uses suffering to drive souls to Himself.
Weariness with the world is often a gateway to heavenly enjoyment, an awakening to higher concerns. The missionary observes that Jesus was a man of sorrows too—what better example
for human emulation? But to avoid the charge that Christianity
is a gloomy religion, he adds that true joy lies in spiritual communion, and he urges the neophyte to seek comfort in Scripture for "all soul cordials are laid up there." Puritan attitudes
about this world and the next were hardly ever better expressed
as when the native preacher observes, "A soul drowned in
earthly pleasure is rarely saved. But a soul drowned in worldly
sorrows and griefs (if influenced in the knowledge of Jesus
Christ) shall never be lost, because the sorrows and crosses of

the world will keep him from surfeiting upon the creature, and
drive him to satiate himself in Christ by the promises of the
gospel."

Having broken with the world, preferring a pilgrim's life
through this vale of tears and temptations, believers could still
suffer doubts about their ultimate fate. Puritans were familiar
with this experience too, even among baptized church members.
So with practiced ease the missionary furnishes advice applicable
to red as well as white penitents. He reminds his imaginary
sachem that salvation is, after all, God's doing. Its chief characteristic is a spiritual rebirth that conveys affected souls into
new life, new perspective. This new birth rarely brings absolute
certainty with it, but believers should trust in God to provide
for their eternal security. That selfless dependence is the best
evidence that grace is truly operating within them and will sustain their journey to ultimate peace. This is the high point of
the dialogue. As an evangelist's manual it properly emphasizes
the early stages of Christian experience. Without implying that
its views present a full survey of Christian life, it tries to deal
with perennial questions troubling those at the threshold of
commitment.

After trying to give his companion what assurance faith can
provide, the missionary urges him to push beyond doubts and
his all too human efforts at self-sufficiency. With typical Calvinist vigor he tells him to trust in God and move on to dutiful
Christian living. Part of salvation's sequence is to put away
worldly attachments, the "outboilings of naughtiness." Moral
rectitude does not make Christians, but it is a necessary com-
ponent in their response to the grace that controls their destiny.
So the missionary patiently explains the process of redemption
as all Puritans understand it, and he presses his convert to en-
graft works of faith onto his soul. If penitents meekly receive
such promises and advice, Eliot was certain that they traveled
the same pathway to salvation as all of God's elect. Through
the mouth of native missionary agents he promises, "This will
save your soul. You are a vessel of grace, and shall be a vessel
of glory. Fear it not. God that cannot lie hath spoken it." The

consequent native response to such pastoral ministration is the
cryptic phrase, "I am another man than I was." This was true
in more ways than probably any of us can fathom.

IV

Training Indian missionaries took time, and the *Dialogues*
contributed substantially to that educative process. Over the
years many natives came to resemble the kind of witness
Eliot depicted in his writings. Several taught regularly in Praying Indian schools; twenty-four served as ordained ministers,
some of them even administering communion to nearby whites
on stated occasions. For a time it seemed as if a burgeoning
native Christianity might gather strength, expand its influence,
and rely increasingly on indigenous leaders. But anticipations
about the future proved to be only speculation because outside
factors interrupted evangelical work soon after Eliot published
his book of dialogues. Events beyond the missionary's control
created a highly detrimental situation that ruined all chances
for what might have been a flourishing native church. War broke
out in 1675 and destroyed all that Eliot had hoped to nurture
in isolated Christian communities.

The downward spiral of red-white relations in New England
had actually begun with diseases introduced before Pilgrims
landed at Plymouth. After that, some colonists tried to deal
fairly with Indians in land purchases and legal administration—
on white terms of course. But on the whole natives resented
rather than appreciated English insistence on uniformity under
their law. White expansionist pressure and diplomatic intrigues
led belligerents of many tribes to rally around the Wampanoag
sachem, Philip, because he symbolized an attempt to save their
cultural autonomy. Philip was not an organizational genius who
designed a pan-Indian alliance capable of pushing all whites back
into the sea. His war started prematurely and was conducted
too sporadically for that. But those who flocked to him suc-
ceeded in waging one of the most devastating and costly wars

in American history. During the conflict known as King Philip's War, half of the white settlements were damaged in fighting, and casualties exceeded 6 percent of the population. By the time Philip was killed in August of 1676, mission work had also been seriously and irreversibly damaged.

Wartime hostilities greatly affected missions by confirming white colonists' latent animosities toward all native Americans. When Wampanoag raiders first struck outlying settlements in Massachusetts and Plymouth, the trouble seemed minor because only one tribe was involved. But various bands of Nipmucks came into the fight too, adding enough manpower to make colonists fear that they were surrounded and outnumbered. Some Nipmucks had come under Puritan influence in the early 1670s, and a few of them had lived for a short while in Christian Indian towns; but most of them joined the Wampanoags in an attempt to end further white encroachment in their territory. All this while, most Massachuset Praying Indians remained peacefully in their towns, even when this docility exposed them to possible attack from marauding Indians. As it turned out, however, they had less to fear from enemy forays than from the siege mentality developing among whites—those whose cause Christian Indians espoused and wished to defend. A few Massachuset warriors left Eliot's missionary reservations to join Philip's forces. Fearful whites blew that evidence out of proportion, concluding that what they had suspected all along was true: no Indian could ever really be trusted. Contagious fears produced a blanket condemnation of all natives, and missionaries could not counteract the anti-Indian feeling that was fed by such wartime hysteria.

Praying Indians and unconverted natives remaining loyal to the whites constituted an estimated one-quarter of the aboriginal population, but indiscriminate racial prejudice did not recognize their worth. Those native forces which were eventually allowed to fight proved to be the key to colonial victory. But even though they were crucial in winning the war, it was impossible to protect loyal natives from white distrust of all their kind. By June 1675, all Praying Indians were ordered to concentrate in five towns "for their own security." Deprived of

weapons and forbidden to hunt, they faced hunger at home
and rejection from whites when they offered to join the war
effort. In October of that year, racial prejudice combined with
wartime panic to produce an extreme measure: the General
Court established what amounted to concentration camps for
loyal Indians. Many fled to escape incarceration, confirming
the suspicions of beleaguered whites. But the friendly accultur-
ated natives, those most willing to internalize English values
and copy alien patterns, submitted to confinement on bleak
Deer Island in Boston Harbor. Eliot, his protégé Daniel Gookin,
and others protested against such harsh tactics, but their words
were in vain and almost resulted in lynching for the old missionary. In the end they could do no more than alleviate some of
the suffering of the natives who made common cause with
their jailers.

Nearly five hundred Praying Indians were forced to endure
the winter of 1675-76 on barren terrain without adequate food,
clothing, or shelter. By late spring colonial authorities relocated
them near Cambridge, but mass incarceration and all its ante-
cedent bullying took a dreadful toll. The prewar mission program
had been crippled, and only four of the old Christian Indian
towns were rebuilt. Missions on Cape Cod and Martha's Vineyard hardly felt the impact of war, and those places absorbed
some Massachuset refugees. But Natick never recovered, counting only 180 residents with ten church members as late as 1698.
Eliot continued to work with the remnant of his converts; but
he was in his seventies by then, and no young missionaries of
his stature emerged to take his place. A reservation system that
lumped belligerents and peaceful Indians together began to super-
sede the old model of havens for cooperative believers. The war
defeated missionary work because it unleashed the pent-up
fears and hostilities most whites had always held against Indians,
converted or not. Christian missionaries had been unable to
allay such prejudices in peacetime; they proved even less effective during the eighteen months of fighting.

The remarkable thing about Puritan oppression of their
faithful friends is that brutalities did not lead Praying Indians
to abandon Christianity altogether. Approximately 40 percent
of the Massachuset converts survived the maelstrom with their

faith intact, however disillusioned they may have become about
their white co-religionists. Their constancy indicates something
of the power with which gospel precepts can sustain individuals
living in a state of grace. But their low residual number graph-
ically highlights the fact that seventeenth-century missions in
New England were irrecoverably broken. Two decades after
the war Eliot's colleagues reported only seven Indian churches
with twenty preaching stations and schools. Natick resisted
attrition better than the other mission towns, but its population
declined to 166 by 1749, to about twenty in 1797, and in 1855
to one Christian Indian. Native converts elsewhere increased
somewhat in the early eighteenth century when the Great
Awakening breathed new life into evangelical work. But native
Christianity never regained its former status in New England
because relentless white expansion increasingly pushed the
dwindling cluster of adherents into cultural oblivion.

V

Anyone examining an original copy of *Indian Dialogues* is
soon struck by two things: it was both hastily written and care-
lessly printed. John Eliot could write clearly. Some of his letters
and a number of his missionary tracts are reasonably clear and
direct. Yet the style and the syntax of the *Dialogues* are anything but straightforward. Anxious to have his handbook quickly available for Indian evangelists, Eliot wrote without much re-
vision. Plainly it was the message that counted, not the literary
expression. Clause piled upon clause, linked by an idiosyncratic
use of semicolons, confront the reader. The seventeenth-century
Indian preachers who sought guidance in the *Dialogues* surely
needed a large measure of patience and perseverence. Eliot's
ideas are sometimes lost in the tangle of run-on sentences and
jumbled paragraphs.

The problem of extracting meaning from the *Dialogues* is
compounded by the especially poor printing done by Marmaduke
Johnson. Johnson was a London printer who emigrated to
Boston in 1660 and worked on Eliot's *Indian Bible* with Samuel

Green. Later Johnson moved to Cambridge, where he established his own press. While Johnson had the newest type in Cambridge, the pages of *Indian Dialogues* are filled nonetheless with inverted letters, broken words, and insufficiently inked lines. The shoddy execution of *Indian Dialogues* may be explained in part by the changing nature of Johnson's business. By the early 1670s the amount of Indian mission work to be printed was decreasing while sermons and theological pamphlets brought to Johnson by patronage from the Mather family was steadily increasing. Perhaps Johnson's business sense told him to spend only a little time on the *Dialogues* and to produce a very limited press run. As a result, the state of the two surviving copies makes any simple facsimile reproduction of the text undesirable.

Faced with existing copies poorly printed and a text of doubtful literary merit, we have followed the advice offered by Samuel Eliot Morison in the Introduction to his edition of William Bradford's *Of Plymouth Plantation.* "My principle in preparing this text," wrote Morison, "is to adopt modern usage as to capitalization, punctuation, and spelling, but scrupulously to respect [the author's] language." By respecting Eliot's language we have sought to clarify its meaning. In an essay for the *Harvard Guide to American History* on editing and printing historical documents, Morison placed considerable emphasis on clarity and consistency. We have chosen to follow generally what Morison called "the expanded method." We have corrected misspellings and typographical errors. To facilitate understanding the sense of the text we have added capital letters when necessary and have provided essential punctuation. In addition, we have employed standard spellings of Indian names and places. At no point have we changed Eliot's language.

It is the content of *Indian Dialogues* that is important. That content reveals as much about Eliot as about his Indian inquirers. The *Dialogues* betray the expectations he acquired in many years of mission experience and are thus revealing in a way that few other pieces of mission literature are. This edition of the *Dialogues* is based on the conviction that what is essential is that this unique work be preserved, explained, and offered to a wider audience.

I N D I A N

Dialogues,

FOR

Their Instruction in that great Service
of Christ, in calling home their
Country-men to the

K nowledge of GOD,

And of THEMSELVES,

AND OF

IESUS CHRIST

Mal. 1:11 *For from the rising of the Sun, even unto the going-
down of the same, my Name shall be great among the
Gentiles, and in every place incense shall be offered
unto my Name, and a pure offering: for my Name shall
be great among the Heathen, saith the Lord of Hosts.*

Printed at Cambridge. 1671

To the Right Worshipful, the Commissioners of the United
Colonies in New England.[1]

Gentlemen,

As I have sometimes said unto you, so I now write, that there
be none on earth that have so great and eminent a calling from
man to take care of the Indians, that they be instructed in the
ways of life by Christ Jesus, as yourselves have. For besides
the Right Honorable Corporation in London,[2] His Majesty our
Sovereign hath ordered a trust to be committed to such as shall
be in your order, namely, Commissioners of the United Colonies
in New England, to take care of this matter. I find few English
students willing to engage into so dim a work as this is. God
hath in mercy raised up sundry among themselves to a com-
petent ability to teach their countrymen. Many have been sent
forth by the church this winter to divers places, and not without good success, through the grace of God: of which I shall
(if God will, and that I live) give you an account at your next
sitting.

I find it necessary for me to instruct them (as in principles of
art, so) in the way of communicating the good knowledge of
God, which I conceive is most familiarly done by way of dialogues; an essay whereunto I do here present unto you: purpos-
ing, if the Lord will, and that I live, to do more of the like kind

hereafter. My earnest request unto yourselves, is, that in all
your respective colonies you would take care that due accom-
modation of lands and waters may be allowed them, where-
upon townships and churches may be (in after ages) able to
subsist; and suffer not the English to strip them of all their
lands, in places fit for the sustenance of the life of man. Thus
commending you to the Lord, I rest,

> Your Worships to serve you in the
> Service of our Lord Jesus
> J. E.

The Preface

These dialogues are partly historical, of some things that were done and said, and partly instructive, to show what might or should have been said, or that may be (by the Lord's assistance) hereafter done and said, upon the like occasion. It is like to be one work incumbent upon our Indian churches and teachers, for some ages, to send forth instruments to call in others from paganry to pray unto God. Instructions therefore of that nature are required, and what way more familiar than by way of dialogues? For sundry weighty reasons I desire and endeavor, that our learned Indians should learn at least the English tongue. If the Lord give life, and length of days, I may hereafter put forth these or the like dialogues in the Indian tongue. But what I shall live to do is known to God. While I live, I desire to follow this work, and serve the Lord with all my might, according to my poor measure and ability, and wait upon the Lord for his blessing, by the concurrent prayers of the faithful.

J. E.

Indian Dialogues

The church did sent forth sundry of the brethren to several parts of the country among their friends and relations, to instruct, exhort and persuade them to pray unto God, to turn from their lewd and lazy life to the living God, and to come forth from the dark dungeon of their lost and ruined condition, into the light of the Lord Jesus, whose glory in the gospel, like the rising sun, beginneth to be displayed among their dead countrymen, who begin to be clothed with sinews, flesh and skin upon their dried bones, by the power of the spirit of Jesus Christ, in the preaching of the gospel unto them.

Piumbukhou[3] was sent to Nashaurreg[4] among his kindred and friends there inhabiting: whose entertainment, discourse and success, was, or is, desired that it might be as followeth.

Near the town a kinsman of his met him; whose discourse was to such purpose as this.

Dialog. I

KINSMAN   PIUMBUKHOU   SPEAKERS

KINSMAN.   Well met, and welcome beloved cousin. I am glad you are still alive. Can you make shift to live in that new way of living that you have taken up at Natick?[5] I am glad of your

coming, because I shall thereby have an opportunity to be informed truly of your ways and what your doings be, about
which there be such various reports, some commending, some
condemning, some deriding, some wondering. But so far as I
see few desire to imitate you.

PIUM.   I am very glad that God hath guided my way so well,
as that I should meet you, whom I have longed to see. You
are my friend whom I purposed first to look out, and lo God
hath ordered us to meet each other, at my first coming to your
town. Likewise I am glad that you are so desirous to speak with
me about our religion, and praying to God, for that is the very
errand I come upon, that I might persuade you to do as we do.
I am like a friend that has found honey, and plenty of food,
and I come to call my friends to come partake with me. But
what noise is this that I hear?

KINSMAN.   I perceive you have quite left off those delights
and fashions that your countrymen use, and which in your
young time accustomed to, because you have forgot the meaning of such noises. There is a great dancing, and sacrifice, and
play, and that is the noise you hear.

PIUM.   You say right. We have indeed quite left off and cast
away those works of darkness. For we have great light shining
among us which discovers the filth and folly of those things;
as when a light is set up in a dark room in a dark night, it dis-
covereth all the dirty corners of the house, and all the evil
actions that are wont to be done in the dark, without discovery.
We plainly see the sinfulness of our own former, and of your
still continued ways, and I desire that God will help me to open
among you some of the divine light which God hath showed us,
that it may shame you from such filthy practices and shine
them away forever, as the rising sun doth dissipate and drive
away all the darkness of the night and maketh wolves, bears,
and all other wild beasts hide themselves in thickets, and not
dare to be seen in the day light.

KINSMAN. Will you go with me unto them, and see what they do? I will give you this one encouragement to persuade you to it, because you shall there see many of your friends and kindred.

PIUM. I cannot serve two masters. I have undertaken and promised to serve God, and therefore I cannot now go back again and serve the Devil. I have found that Jesus Christ is a good master, and I come to persuade you to come and be his servant. Far be it from me that now I am come among you, I should forsake my master, and serve the Devil; or that I should so far grieve my master, as to go unto those games, which his soul hateth.

And whereas you say, that many of my friends are there, the more is my grief. I desire that I were able to pull you all out of that deep pit and filthy puddle; which to perform, I should utterly be disabled, if I should go in myself, and so be defiled with the same filth, which I persuade them to forsake and cast away.

KINSMAN. Let us go unto my house, that you make take there some refreshment of food after your weary journey, and there we shall have liberty to discourse fully of these matters. And while we are in the way, let me ask you of the estate and welfare of our friends and kindred at Natick. Doth your praying to God exempt you from sickness, poverty, nakedness? Will praying to God fill you with food, gladness, and garments?

PIUM. Our friends at Natick were when I left them in good state of health, peace, and comfort: for which we give God thanks, who is the father of all mercies.

Touching your question, whether praying to God doth exempt us from sickness, poverty, and fills us with food and garments. I answer, if praying to God did bring with it outward plenty and worldly prosperity, then all carnal people would pray to God, not because they love God, or praying to God, but because they love themselves, and love food, clothing, and worldly pleasures. But the benefits of praying are spiritual and

heavenly, it teaches us to know God, and the evil of sin; it
teacheth us to repent of sin, and seek for pardon, and it teacheth us to forsake sin forever. And if we are loth to part with sin,
God will chastise us with sickness, poverty, and other worldly
crosses, to call us to repentance, and therefore many times we
fare worse in the world then wicked men do, that thereby we
might be weaned from the world and brought and taught to
love and long for heaven. And yet I further tell you, that
religion doth teach the right way to be rich and prosperous
in this world, and many, English especially, have learned that
way. For religion teacheth us to be diligent in labor six days,
and on the seventh day to rest, and keep it an holy sabbath;
and God hath promised that *the diligent hand shall make rich.*[6]
And when we walk with God in godliness and obedience, he
will give us the blessing of this life, so far as it best for us. He
will withhold no good thing from us. If any thing be withheld
from us, or taken away from us, it is because it is not good for
us. Our father better knoweth what is good for us, then we ourselves know.

KINSMAN. If your praying to God do indeed teach you the
true way of being rich, as you say, how then cometh it to pass
you are so poor still? For you have prayed to God these twenty
years and more, and I do not see that you have increased in
riches very much. You are still poor. Where are your riches?
Where be your flocks and herds of cattle? Where be your
clothes? What great houses have you built? Where be your
fields of corn, barns and orchards? Alas, you are not like the
English; and therefore I doubt upon this point. It is not as you
say, that praying to God teacheth you the right way to be rich.

PIUM. This is one of the least, the last, the lowest of those
things that our religion teacheth us. There be two sorts of riches;
earthly riches, of which only you speak, and heavenly riches,
which God's word calleth true riches. These earthly riches are
but temporary, and shall soon perish. But the true riches are
heavenly, and eternal. They last forever. And we have spent
these twenty years in seeking chiefly after heavenly riches, for

so God commandeth us in his word, *Seek first the kingdom of heaven.* As for these earthly riches, *they shall be added to you,* so much as you need. And the word of God commandeth us to *be content if we have food and clothes.*[7] Now we have food and clothes more then we were wont to have before we prayed to God, and we have contented ourselves therewith, and have bent our minds more to look after heavenly riches, and in those things we have increased more, than in earthly riches.

KINSMAN. I pray tell me what are those heavenly riches of which you speak so highly, and upon which you bestow your chief care and pains, and so much prefer before earthly riches, which we account so much of, and think to be the best things attainable in this world?

PIUM. The true riches which we spend our time to seek after, are, 1. The knowledge of the great God, who hath made this vast world, and governeth the same by his wisdom and power, and who hath made man, and governeth us by his holy laws and commandments. 2. The knowledge of ourselves, who be miserable sinners, and do daily offend and sin against God, provoking his wrath against us, to punish us for our transgressions against his holy laws and commandments. 3. The knowledge of Jesus Christ, the Redeemer of the world, who hath in unspeakable love took a course to deliver us from the wrath of God. For whereas we have by our sins deserved death and damnation, Christ became a man, and died for us, and thereby hath pacified the justice and wrath of God, and opened a way of salvation for us, obtaining a pardon for us, and offering grace unto us, whereby we may be saved, and be brought to eternal glory and happiness. 4. The knowledge of the grace of God in Jesus Christ, whereby he bringeth us to repent of our sins, to convert and turn from all our evil ways, and to believe in the Lord Jesus, and to walk with God in the ways of holiness and righteousness before him. 5. The knowledge of the means of grace, the ordinances of God; whereby we walk with God in ways of civil government, and good order. And in the ordinances of worshipping God, in the sanctifying of the sabbath, and walk-

ing in the communion of saints, by the Word of God, and
prayer, and singing of Psalms. 6. In the knowledge of the estate
of all men after death; how the godly men that penitently believe in Christ, go to heaven when they die; and the wicked,
that refuse to repent and believe, they go to hell, and there
abide till the day of judgement; at which day or time, when it
cometh, all men shall rise again and be judged according to their
deeds in this life. And then shall the godly go with Christ to
eternal glory, and the wicked shall be cast into hell, soul and
body, and there be tormented with the devils forever.

KINSMAN.   These are great and strange things you speak of. I
understand them not. But yet methinks there is a majesty and
glory in them. I am amazed at what you say, though I do not
understand them distinctly.

PIUM.   You see then that we are grown rich with riches that
are above your capacity; and these are the *true riches*, and
about these things we spend most of our time. And as for these
worldly riches, we less regard them, as being poor, low, little,
small, contemptible things, in comparison of those heavenly
riches about which we spend our time, and in which we have
increased and gained, by God's grace in Christ, so much as doth
make you admire at us, though we know but little of what is
to be known, but you cannot perceive the glory and excellency
thereof.

   And indeed it is the wisdom and love of God unto us, that
setteth us rather to grow in these riches, which the eyes of
worldly men cannot see, than to grow rich in earthly and worldly riches, which the carnal world can see. Because if we should
abound in earthly riches, we should be thronged with multi-
tudes of carnal persons, who love the world, and love not God,
who would be a cumber and temptation to us. And it is a sign
that our ways are good and godly, and above the world, because so few (in comparison) come unto us, but rather fly from
us; because they love to live in ways and deeds of darkness, and
hate the light and glory that is in our ways. But I pray cousin,
whose house that is before us, where I see so many going in
and out, and standing about in every place?

KINSMAN. That is my house, and I am glad there be so many of our friends together, who may have the opportunity to hearing this good discourse.

[After their entrance into the house, there be four speakers: Kinsman, Kinswoman, All the Company, Piumbukhou]

KINSMAN. I had rather that my actions of love should testify how welcome you are, and how glad I am of this your kind visitation, than that I should say it in a multitude of words. But in one word, you are very welcome into my heart, and I account it among the best of the joys of this day, that I see your face, and enjoy your company in my habitation.

KINSWOMAN. It is an addition to the joys of this day, to see the face of my loving kinsman. And I wish you had come a little earlier, that you might have taken part with us in the joys of this day, wherein we have had all the delights that could be desired, in our merry meeting, and dancing.

And I pray cousin, how doth your wife, my loving kinswoman, is she yet living? And is she not yet weary of your new way of praying to God? And what pleasure have you in those ways?

PIUM. My wife doth remember her love to you. She is in good health of body, and her soul is in a good condition. She is entered into the light of the knowledge of God, and of Christ. She is entered into the narrow way of heavenly joys, and she doth greatly desire that you would turn from these ways of darkness in which you so much delight, and come taste and see how good the Lord is.

And whereas you wish I had come sooner, to have shared with you in your delights of this day. Alas, they are no delights, but griefs to me, to see that you do still delight in them. I am like a man that have tasted of sweet wine and honey, which have so altered the taste of my mouth, that I abhor to taste of your sinful and foolish pleasures, as the mouth doth abhor to taste the most filthy and stinking dung, the most sour grapes, or most bitter gall. Our joys in the knowledge of God, and of

Jesus Christ, which we are taught in the Book of God, and feel in our heart, is sweeter to our soul, than honey is unto the mouth and taste.

KINSWOMAN.   We have all the delights that the flesh and blood of man can devise and delight in, and we taste and feel the delights of them, and would you make us believe that you have found out new joys and delights, in comparison of which all our delights do stink like dung? Would you make us believe that we have neither eyes to see, nor ears to hear, nor mouth to taste? Ha, ha, he! I appeal to the sense and sight and feeling of the company present, whether this be so.

ALL.   You say very true. Ha, ha, he!

PIUM.   Hearken to me, my friends, and see if I do not give a clear answer unto this seeming difficulty. Your dogs take as much delight in these meetings, and the same kinds of delight as you do. They delight in each others company. They provoke each other to lust, and enjoy the pleasures of lust as you do. They eat and play and sleep as you do. What joys have you more than dogs have to delight the body of flesh and blood?

But all mankind have an higher and better part than the body. We have a soul, and that soul shall never die. Our soul is to converse with God, and to converse in such things as do concern God, and heaven, and an eternal estate, either in happiness with God, if we walk with him and serve him in this life, or in misery and torment with the Devil, if we serve him in this life. The service of God doth consist in virtue, and wisdom, and delights of the soul, which will reach to heaven, and abide forever.

But the service of the Devil is in committing sins of the flesh, which defile both body and soul, and reach to hell, and will turn all to fire and flame to torment your souls and bodies in all eternity.

Now consider, all your pleasures and delights are such as defile you with sin, and will turn to flame, to burn and torment you. They provoke God to wrath, who hath created the prison of hell to torment you, and the more you have took pleasure

in sin, the greater are your offences against God, and the greater shall be your torments.

But we that pray to God repent of our old sins, and by faith
in Christ we seek for, and find a pardon for what is past, and
grace and strength to reform for time to come. So that our joys
are soul joys in godliness, and virtue, and hope of glory in another world when we die.

Your joys are bodily, fleshly, such as dogs have, and will all
turn to flames in hell to torment you.

KINSMAN. If these things be so, we had need to cease laugh-
ing, and fall to weeping, and see if we can draw water from our
mournful eyes to quench these tormenting flames. My heart
trembles to hear these things. I never heard so much before,
nor have I any thing to say to the contrary, but that these
things may be so. But how shall I know that you say true?
Our forefathers were (many of them) wise men, and we have
wise men now living. They all delight in these our delights. They
have taught us nothing about our soul, and God, and heaven,
and hell, and joy and torment in the life to come. Are you wiser
than our fathers? May not we rather think that *English* men
have invented these stories to amaze us and fear us out of our
old customs, and bring us to stand in awe of them, that they
might wipe us of our lands, and drive us into corners, to seek
new ways of living, and new places too? And be beholding to
them for that which is our own, and was ours, before we knew
them.

ALL. You say right.

PIUM. The Book of God is no invention of Englishmen. It is
the holy law of God himself, which was given unto man by God,
before Englishmen had any knowledge of God; and all the
knowledge which they have, they have it out of the Book of
God. And this book is given to us as well as to them, and it is
as free for us to search the scriptures as for them. So that we
have our instruction from a higher hand, than the hand of man.
It is the great Lord God of heaven and earth, who teacheth us

these great things of which we speak. Yet this is also true, that
we have great cause to be thankful to the English, and to thank
God for them. For they had a good country of their own, but
by ships sailing into these parts of the world, they heard of us,
and of our country, and of our nakedness, ignorance of God,
and wild condition. God put it into their hearts to desire to
come hither, and teach us the good knowledge of God; and their
King gave them leave so to do, and in our country to have their
liberty to serve God according to the word of God. And being
come hither, we gave them leave freely to live among us. They
have purchased of us a great part of those lands which they
possess. They love us, they do us right, and no wrong willingly.
If any do us wrong, it is without the consent of their rulers,
and upon our complaints our wrongs are righted. They are
(many of them, especially the ruling part) good men, and desire to do us good. God put it into the heart of one of their
ministers (as you all know) to teach us the knowledge of God,
by the word of God, and hath translated the holy Book of
God into our language,[8] so that we can perfectly know the
mind and counsel of God. And out of this book have I learned
all that I say unto you, and therefore you need no more doubt
of the truth of it, then you have cause to doubt that the heaven
is over our head, the sun shineth, the earth is under our feet,
we walk and live upon it, and breathe in the air. For as we see
with our eyes these things to be so, so we read with our own
eyes these things which I speak of, to be written in God's own
book, and we feel the truth thereof in our own hearts.

KINSWOMAN.   Cousin, you have wearied your legs this day
with a long journey to come and visit us, and you weary your
tongue with long discourses. I am willing to comfort and re-
fresh you with a short supper.

ALL.   Ha, ha, he. Though short, if sweet that has good favor
to a man that is weary. Ha, ha, he.

KINSWOMAN.   You make long and learned discourses to us
which we do not well understand. I think our best answer is to

stop your mouth, and fill your belly with a good supper, and when your belly is full you will be content to take rest yourself, and give us leave to be at rest from these gastering[9] and heart-trembling discourses. We are well as we are, and desire not to be troubled with these new wise sayings.

ALL. You say true. Ha, ha, he.

PIUM. It is good to be merry and wise. I am hungry and weary, and willing to eat. God hath appointed food to be a means of sustaining, relieving and repairing our spent strength. This being a work above the power of the food we eat, or of ourselves that eat it, and only in the power of God himself to bless it, for such great uses. Therefore God hath taught us, and it is our custom, among all that are godly, to pray to God for a blessing before we eat and therefore I entreat you to have so much patience and compliance, as to give me the quiet liberty to pray to God before we eat.

KINSMAN. I pray do, and we shall with quietness and silence attend to such a service unto God.

PIUM. Let us lift up our eyes and hearts to God in heaven, and say, almighty, glorious, merciful and heavenly Father, thou dwellest in the high heavens, and fillest both heaven and earth with thy presence. Thou takest care of, and governest us here on earth. We are poor worms under thy feet, thou feedest every living creature, and makest our food to be like a staff to sustain our faint and weary bodies. Thou renewest our strength every day and though we are sinners in thy sight, yet thou art merciful to us, and with long patience dost call us to repentance. We confess all our sins before thee, and pray thee for Jesus Christ, his sake, who died for sinners, to have mercy on us, and freely pardon and forgive us all our sins. Bless us at this time, and this food which is set before us. Let it be blessed to us. Make us wise to receive it at thy hand, and to use the strength we get by it to the glory of thy name, through Jesus Christ. And bless all our souls, feed them by thy word and

truth, and guide our tongues to speak wise words, that may
minister grace to the hearers, and help us all to rejoice in the
Lord through Jesus Christ. Amen. Now let us eat and rejoice
together, for God filleth our bodies with food, and our souls
with gladness.

KINSMAN.   When the body is full of meat, and the head full of
wit, and the mouth full of words, there will be wise discourse.

PIUM.   Add but one more thing. *If the heart be full of grace*,
then the discourse will be both wise and godly.[10]

ALL.   Ha, ha, he. They be not half full yet. Ha, ha, he.

KINSMAN.   What news do the ships bring from beyond sea?

PIUM.   They say wicked men are bold, and that good men who
pray to God are hated, vexed, troubled, persecuted, and not
suffered to pray to God according to the laws of God's word,
but by the laws of men.

ALL.   It is an ill time for you to come to persuade us to pray
to God, when praying to God is so opposed, hated, and hindered.
You may be more like to prevail with us, when praying to God
is of credit, honor, and good esteem.

PIUM.   Such as will turn to God only at such times when praying is in credit, leave themselves under a doubt, whether it be
for the love of God and his ways, that they pray, or for the
love of themselves and their own credit.
   But when men will take up praying to God in evil times,
when they must expect hard measure from the world for it,
this is a sign that they love God, and love praying to God, better
then they love themselves, and that they deny themselves, for
Christ his sake. Therefore I have taken the fittest time to try
you, and to sift you, to catch none but the good corn, and to
let go and lose all the dust and chaff.

KINSMAN. Some speak of very many English people killed with thunder, and many burnt in their houses. Is it so indeed?

PIUM. It is so indeed, and in many parts of the country, at Boston, and in many other places. Very lately, there were in one winter eight or nine persons burnt to death in one house, five in another, one in another. Sicknesses are often sent of God among them, which kill many. Their corn is blasted, and they are punished by God many ways, by sea and land, in these late years.[11]

KINSWOMAN. These are but cold and weak arguments to persuade us to take up the English fashion, and to serve their God, when you tell us how sharply he dealt with his servants.

ALL. You say right. We are better as we are.

PIUM. We know there be many sins among the English, which provoke God to be angry with them, and to punish them, to the end he might bring them to repentance. When we exhort you to pray, and to serve the God of the English, we call you to imitate the virtues and good ways of the English, wherein you shall be acceptable to the Lord. We do not call you to imitate their sins, whereby they and you shall provoke the anger and displeasure of the Lord. And what though God doth chastise his people for their sins? It is his wisdom, faithfulness, and love so to do. A child will not run away from his wise and loving father, because he chastises him for his faults, but will love him the better, fear him the more, and learn thereby to be a good child. The wise English love God the more, for his wise chastisement of them for their sins. And why may not I use it as an argument to persuade you to choose him to be your God, who will love and encourage you in all virtue, and love and punish you for all sins, that he might bring you to repentance and amendment of life. God's rods have more encouragement to a wise heart than discouragement to them.

KINSWOMAN.   Cousin, had you not a great thunder and light-
ning today as you came, and were you not afraid? We had it so
with us, and I was very much afraid, and especially since I have
heard of so many English stricken and killed by it, and cannot
restrain myself from fear.

PIUM.   I perceived the thunder to be more this way, than it
was in the place where I was at that time travelling. Touching
the fear of thunder, the word of God saith it is terrible, and
the brute beasts tremble at it. It is sometime called *The Voice
of God*, by reason of the terribleness of it. And the reason of
its terror to man is, because we are great sinners, and have deserved God's wrath, and it should move our hearts to repentance
for our sins, and take heed of provoking the anger of that God,
who is able to utter so terrible a voice, and can dash down
destroying fire upon us worms, who are no ways able to defend
our selves.

KINSMAN.   Would you not lie down now you have eaten, and
take some rest after your long journey?

PIUM.   Nay, we must first return to God, and give thanks to
him for our food, and health and strength by the same.

KINSMAN.   I pray tell me why you are so careful to pray unto
God before and after meat?

PIUM.   Let us first give thanks, and then we will discourse that
point. Attend all. We do give humble thanks unto thy holy
name, O Lord our God, for our life, health, food, raiments,
and for the present food whereby we are refreshed. We thank
thee, O Lord, for the love we find among our friends, and for
our freedom in good discourse for the good of our souls. We
do pray for a blessing upon both, that our food may strengthen
our bodies, and our discourse may do good to our souls. Help
me so to declare thy word and thy works, that I may win their
souls to love thee, and to forsake their sins, and turn unto the

Lord by true repentance. These, and all other mercies we pray
for, in the name, and for the sake of our Lord Jesus Christ. Amen.

ALL.   Tabat, tabat, tabat.[12]

PIUM.   Now my kinsmen and friends, let us discourse a little
about the question propounded, why we pray unto God before
and after meat? Our Lord Jesus Christ did so before meat, as
it is written of him in many examples, and we are not to doubt
but he did the same after meat, because the Lord hath commanded the same so expressly, saying, *when thou hast eaten
and art full, then beware lest thou forget the Lord.*[13]

And to show you what great reason we have thus to do, consider that God doth some of his chief works in this world, in
the matter of our eating, which no creature can do. For take
you a tray of meat, and ask, who can turn this into blood, and
flesh, and sinews, and bones, and skin? And who can give every
part of our body its due proportion, that one part shall not
overgrow the other, but every part alike? Who but God can do
this? And who but God can make our bodies grow to such an
appointed stature, and then to grow no more? And who but
God can preserve our health and turn away sickness? Now these
marvelous things God doth for us every day, and every time we
eat, and therefore is it not very good reason that we should pray
and give thanks to God at such time as he doth such great and
obliging things for us?

Again, God provideth all our food for us. He provideth corn,
not we ourselves. We do but a little towards it. The great work
is God's. All that we do is to put our corn into the ground,
and keep the ground clean about it, but God makes it grow. He
gives it a root, a blade, a stalk, and ears, whereby one corn
shall become three or four or five hundred. Who but God can
do this? Therefore corn is of his providing.

Again, who provideth water, and watereth the corn? Is it not
God? For when springs and rivers are dried up, what can men
do, but cry to God? And then God will bring clouds, like great
bottles full of water, and drop them down upon the withered

and parched earth, and thereby make the corn and grass and
all fruits to grow. Who but God can do this?

Again, God provides flesh for us to feed upon, for he maketh
the grass and herbs to grow, and when the beasts do feed there-
on, he doth turn those leaves into blood, flesh, sinews and
bones, and this he giveth us for food, and turneth it into blood,
flesh, sinews, and bones in us. All these wonderful works God
doth, in the matter of feeding us, and therefore is it not good
reason we should then pray to him?

KINSMAN.   I never heard so much before, nor thought of these
things. But now you declare and teach them, my heart saith,
that all is true which you say, and I now see great reason for
this practice of you that pray to God, to pray and give thanks
both before and after meat. And I see not but that there is
good and just reason so to do, every time we drink, and take
any sustenance, at least to lift up our hearts to God, who hath
so eminent an hand in doing us good thereby, or hurt if he will.

PIUM.   Your acceptance and approbation of what I say, and of
what we do in this point, is a great argument that God doth bow
your heart to pray unto God. For you acknowledge it to be
our duty so to do, and the neglect of it would be against the
light of your own reason, so that this conviction hath cast a
chain upon your soul, to bind you to pray unto God. What say
you my friends?

ALL.   We cannot say any thing against what you say, but what
we shall do, we cannot yet tell. We must first consider of it,
for we are ignorant and foolish. We cannot do as you do.

PIUM.   Bend your hearts to it, and God will teach you by his
word. For we were at first as ignorant as you are, but God
helped us to hear the word, and do what we could, and you
see what God hath brought the matter unto. We now walk in
the light, and now we call you to come into the light. Therefore I say, *awake you that sleep, stand up from the dead, and
Christ will give you light.*[14]

KINSMAN.   We shall tire you with these discourses after your long and weary journey. It is time for you to go to rest.

PIUM.   This discourse is better to me than meat, drink and sleep, if I may do good to your souls, and turn you unto God.

But before we go to rest and sleep, we must pray unto God, for it is God that giveth rest and sleep unto his servants.

KINSMAN.   Do all you praying Indians thus do when you are weary and tired with labor, or travel, or hunting, etc.? Do you pray before you go to rest? What is the reason of your so doing?

PIUM.   We always do so, and if any should at any time through sloth or sleepiness fail so to do, we judge ourselves for our sin, and repent, and confess our sin unto God, and beg pardon and mercy for Christ his sake.

And there is great reason thus to pray unto God before we go to rest. For besides what I said that God giveth us rest, and therefore it is fit humbly to ask it of him, there be many other reasons why we should thus do: for 1. We must give God thanks for all the mercies we have received all the day, which are more than the moments of the time that we live. 2. We must pray for God's protection of us when we are asleep. We lie like so many dead men, and how easily might mischief befall us, either by fire, or by an enemy, if God did not defend and keep us. But when God is our keeper we may rest quietly, in safety without fear, under the covert[15] of his hand. And by faith in God's protection we sleep quietly without fear, whereas you that do not pray, nor believe, nor commit your selves to God, you do always sleep in fear and terror. 3. Moreover, our sleep and rest is a great reparation of our strength and spirits, and preservation of our health. While we sleep our food is boiled up within us, and digested into all parts of our body, and new spirits are extracted out of our food, and sent up both to our head, heart, and all parts of our body, so that we are fresh and strong in the morning after a good night's rest. Now all this is the special work of God, beyond the power and skill of man to perform for us, and therefore it is great reason to pray for this blessing when we go to rest.

KINSMAN. What you say is plain, clear and true in every bodies experience, though I never heard nor considered so much of it before. If therefore you will pray we will attend you.

PIUM. Let us appear before God reverently and with godly fear. Let none lie along or sit, which are postures of unreverence, but either stand like servants, or kneel like sons and daughters before the Lord. And so let us pray. *O merciful Lord God*, etc.

KINSMAN. I perceive that you pray for all our countrymen, who do not yet pray unto God. It is your love so to do. But what is the effect of your prayers? There are not many, that I hear of, that pray unto God. And you that do pray unto God, what do you get by it? Wherein are you bettered by your praying to God?

PIUM. These are two great points which you have propounded. I am willing to speak to both. First, for the numbers that pray to God. At first this matter of praying to God was a little thing, like a cloud in the west of the bigness of a man's hand. But now the cloud is great and wide, and spreadeth over all the country. Nop,[16] and Nantuket,[17] and Paumenuk islands,[18] Mahshepog,[19] and many parts of the mainland to the utmost bounds of this country eastward. And westward, not only all the Massachusets[20] pray, but also a large part of Nipmuk.[21] Yea and the fields are ripe unto the harvest in many places more, whom I will not name until they have given up themselves to the Lord, to forsake their vanities, and to pray unto God. The church at Natick have sent forth many into many parts of the country, to call them in unto Jesus Christ. I am sent unto you, and I have good hope that God will bow your hearts to pray unto God. So that the *praying Indians* are many, and like to be more every year. And our hope is the greater, because the Lord hath raised up sundry of our young men (who were children when we first prayed unto God) unto good knowledge in the scriptures, and are able to teach others the good knowledge of God, and are fit to be sent forth unto all parts of the country, to teach them to pray unto God.

KINSWOMAN.   Husband, what do you mean to withhold our friend from rest so long, so late? Alas cousin, you had need to be at rest. I pray tire not yourself with these long discourses.

PIUM.   I thank you for your care of me. There is but one thing more that I am to speak to, viz. the second part of your question, *what have we gained and got by praying to God?* Of which point we discoursed before we came into the house, and therefore I shall but touch on it now.

  1. We are come into the light, and it is an heavenly light, which leadeth us to God, and to the eternal enjoyment of happiness by Jesus Christ.

  2. We have attained to some measure of the true riches, by faith in Jesus Christ, and love to God and his people.

  3. We are content with that portion of food and raiment which God giveth us.

  4. We enjoy the Lord's Sabbath days for our souls good, and communion with God.

  5. We have government, and all God's ordinances in peace.

  6. We can lie down in peace, and sleep quietly without fear.

In all which, and many more respects, our condition doth far exceed what we were and had afore we prayed to God, or what you have or enjoy unto this day. And now let us lie down in God's bosom, and take our rest.

Next Morning
KINSMAN KINSWOMAN PIUMBUKHOU

KINSMAN.   Are you well this morning? Have you slept well this night? Doth not your weary journey lie in your bones? Is not the skin of your feet that was worn thin with rocks and rough ways still tender?

PIUM.   By the mercy of God through Jesus Christ, I am every way well refreshed. The comfort of my soul doth make my bodily infirmities inconsiderable. And that which addeth much to the comfort of my soul, is the good attention which you and some other of our friends gave unto our discourse and prayers the last night, which giveth me hope *that you are not far from the kingdom of God.*

KINSMAN.   I confess my thoughts have troubled me this night. I have a great strife in my heart. I think your way is right. I cannot gainsay any thing of which you discoursed. But on the other side, if I should forsake our former ways, all my friends would rise up against me like a stream too strong for me to stand against, and I am not able to defend myself against them. I do not know what to do.

PIUM.   God is above man. When I began to pray to God, I had the same temptation, but I quickly found how vain and weak it was. God will defend all his servants against all gainsayers. The light and power of God's word and ways will soon shame all sinners into silence.

But I will tell you a further help in this case. We shall endeavor to convince and persuade all your friends to turn unto God also, and then that temptation will quite sink. Let us therefore get your friends and neighbors together, and labor to persuade them all first to hear the word of God preached among you. And my hope is that God will persuade so many of them, as that the rest will be ashamed to oppose. For darkness and sin are weak, truth and light are powerful.

KINSWOMAN.   My thoughts have also troubled me this night. But if you shall take that course, then I shall gladly join with my husband in this change. I will therefore get you some victuals to eat, and then to go about that business.

PIUM.   We are not ready for eating yet. We must first go to prayer, and give God thanks for his mercies the night past, and this morning, and we will pray unto God for his blessings all this day, and pray that he would bless our endeavours to persuade them. For the hearts of all men are in God's hand, and he can overcome them and persuade them.

KINSMAN. I like well what you say. I pray therefore do so. We will attend and join with you.

PIUM. Let us humbly bow our knees and hearts before the all-seeing God, and in the name of Jesus Christ pray unto him. But there come some company. Let them first come in. It may be they will join with us in our prayers.

KINSMAN. A good morning to you my friends. You come in a good season. Our friend is come from far to visit us, and attend unto what he prayeth.

ALL. We shall willingly keep silence and attend.

PIUM. Prayeth ——.

KINSMAN. This good friend of ours is come to visit us, and doth persuade us to pray unto God, and you hear how heartily he prayeth unto God for us. What think you of it?

ALL. We cannot tell. We do not yet understand the matter. How then should we answer to it?

KINSMAN. Your answer is right and discreet. Let us therefore discourse about this matter. Wise men will look before they leap.

ALL. We are but a few, and weak men. Let us send for the sachem,[22] and the rest of the old and wise men, and especially for the pauwau,[23] and then let us discourse of such matters. They better know what to say in these matters than we do.

KINSWOMAN. I like the motion. And I pray you in the mean time eat such food as I have prepared for you, that when they come together, you may be ready without interruption, to attend unto what you are purposed to do.

PIUM. Always before we eat we must pray. The last night I gave you some reasons for it by the word of God, and seeing

here be more of our friends come in, who heard not our discourse last night, I will again rehearse the same or the like
reasons for this religious practice. He discourseth them ——.

KINSWOMAN.   Your meat is ready. If therefore you will please
to pray, according as you wisely discourse, I hope we shall all
attend.

ALL.   We shall attend.

PIUM.   Prayeth for a blessing ——.

KINSWOMAN.   Cousin, I am glad to see you eat so heartily.
You are very welcome to it. And I see that praying to God
doth not fill your bellies. You need food for all that.

ALL.   Ha, ha, he. Praying to God would starve them if they
should not eat. Ha, ha, he. Praying Indians are as weary and
hungry as other men, for ought we ever saw by them. Ha, ha, he.

PIUM.   It is true what you say, and therefore we pray unto God
to give us food, and to bless it to us when we eat it.
    This discourse bringeth to my mind a word which Christ
spake. Man liveth not by bread alone, but by every word of
God.[24] Man hath two parts, a soul, and a body, and both are to
be fed. The body is fed by food, the soul is fed by the word of
God, and prayer. You that pray not to God, you feed your
bodies only. But you starve your souls. We that pray to God
feed our souls as well as our bodies. And this is one reason why
we persuade you to pray to God, because we would not have
you to starve your souls. The soul is the most excellent part of
man, and shall never die. The body shall die. If you have so
much wisdom as to feed your bodies, we pray you be yet more
wise, and feed your souls also.

KINSMAN.   Everything that liveth doth live by feeding, as birds,
beasts, fishes, and so do men.

PIUM. You say true, and the souls of men are living souls, and therefore should be fed with the food which God hath appointed for them, and that is the word of God and prayer.

KINSMAN. If our souls be living souls, what do they feed upon? We having neither the word of God nor prayer.

PIUM. Your souls feed upon nothing but lust, and lying, and stealing, and killing, and sabbath-breaking, and pauwauing. And all these are sins which poison, starve, and kill your souls, and expose them to God's wrath that they may be tormented among devils and wicked men in hell fire forever. And therefore it is in love to your souls that we persuade you to pray unto God. But now that we have eaten and are sufficed with food, let us give thanks to God for it, and pray that it may be blessed to us. [He giveth thanks]

KINSMAN. Yonder come a great company of our friends. Order the house against they come.

KINSMAN SACHEM PAUWAU PIUM. ALL

KINSMAN. Welcome sontim.[25] Welcome my friends and kinsmen all. Here is a kinsman and friend of ours come from Natick to visit us. He prayeth for us, and expresseth love to our souls, which you take no thought or care about. He telleth us of light and wisdom which they learn out of the Word of God, which we are strangers unto. He telleth us of hell fire and torments, to be the reward of our sins, which we walk in. He telleth us of repentance for our sins, and of faith to believe in Christ for a pardon, and of salvation in heaven with eternal glory. He telleth us of the danger of living as we do. He telleth us of a better way of living than yet we know. Many such things we have discoursed, which are beyond my understanding. I am well pleased with his love. But I know not what to say to his persuasions, for which cause I have entreated your company, that we may confer together about matters of so great importance, and that we may be mutual helps to each other for our best good.

SONT.   If any man bring us a precious jewel, which will make us rich and happy, everybody will make that man welcome, and if this friend of ours do that, who more welcome? But if by receiving his jewel, we must part with a better jewel for it, then wise men should do well to consider, before they accept his offer. These things you speak of are great things. But if we accept of them, consider what we must part with and forego for ever; viz., all your pleasures and sports, and delights and joys in this world.

ALL.   You say true. Ha, ha, he.

PIUM.   If foolish youths play in the dirt, and eat dung, and stinking fish and flesh, and rotten corn for company's sake, their sachem makes this law: if you come forth from that filthy place and company, and feed upon this wholesome and good food I have provided, then you shall be honoured and well used all your life time. But if you so love your old company, as that you choose rather to feed on trash, and venture to perish among them, then perish you shall, and thank yourself for your foolish choice. This was our case at first, and is yours to this day. You walk in darkness, defile yourselves with a filthy conversation, you feed your souls with trash and poison, and you choose to do so for your company's sake. Behold, God calls you to come out from among them, and touch no unclean thing, to converse among the wise, and offereth you pardon, life, and salvation in heaven, in glory, among all the elect, saints and angels. Now you are at your choice. Will you forsake those bad courses and companions, and live in glory? Or will you choose your old filthy courses and companions, and perish forever?

SONT.   All our forefathers (so far as ever we have heard) have walked and lived as we do, and are we wiser than our fathers?

PIUM.   No, we are foolish, weak and sinful and love to be vile.
But God is wiser than our fathers, and he hath opened to us
this way of wisdom and life, and calleth us to enter, and walk
therein. Therefore be wise, and submit your selves to the call
of Christ.

SONT.   But why do you say that we feed upon trash, stinking
meat and poison? Wherein doth our food differ from yours,
and wherein do you in that respect excel us?

PIUM.   In bodily food we differ not from you. But it is soul
food I speak of. We feed our souls with the word of God and
prayer. You feed and satiate your souls with lust, lying, stealing, sabbath-breaking, and such like sins. And I appeal to your
own conscience, whether these are not trash and filthiness,
and what fruit can you expect from such actions, but punishment and wrath?

PAUWAU.   Let me add a few words to give check to your high-
flown confidence to your new way, and new laws, and to your
deep censoriousness of our old ways, the pleasancy and delight
whereof everyone, both man, woman, and child, can judge of.
And we cannot but dislike to have such pleasant delights taken
from us. Tear our hair from our heads, our skin from our flesh,
our flesh from our bones, you shall as soon persuade us to suffer
you to do by us, as to persuade us to part with our old delights
and courses. You tell us of the Englishman's God, and of his
laws. We have Gods also, and more than they. And we have
laws also by which our forefathers did walk, and why should
not we do as they have done? To change our Gods, and laws,
and customs, are great things, and not easily to be obtained
and accomplished. Let us alone, that we may be quiet in the
ways which we like and love, as we let you alone in your changes
and new ways.

ALL.   You say right. Why trouble they us in our pleasures and
delights? Let us alone in our enjoyments.

PIUM.   You have spoken many things, which do minister matter
to me of much discourse, both concerning God, and our selves,
and concerning you, and the offer of God's mercy to you at
this time. You say you have many gods, but they are no gods.
There is but one God, the great creator of this great world.
Did your gods make this world, the heavens, the sun, the moon,
the stars, the clouds, the seas, and the whole earth? No, no.
God made this whole world. Can any of your gods give rain,
or rule the clouds? It is the Devil that blindeth your eyes, and
covereth you with darkness. We teach you to know the true
God, who can kill us, or keep us alive at his pleasure. Your
gods shall all perish with you, for they are no gods.

As for your pleasures and delights, they are all sins against
God, which provoke his wrath to plague you forever. We now
call you to repent of your evil ways, and to reform your lives
to serve the true and living God, to seek for pardon of your
sins, and mercy to appease his wrath which is kindled against
you. I do now offer you mercy through Jesus Christ. Do not
harden your hearts against the Lord. Be therefore persuaded
now to forsake your sins and turn unto the Lord. Come unto
the light out of your darkness. Awake from your dead sleep,
stand up, and Christ will give you life. We speak by experience.
We were dead and blind as you are. We loved pleasures as you
do, but by the grace of Christ we have found light and life,
and now call you to partake with us in our mercies.

PAUWAU.   We have not only our pleasures, but also prayers and
sacrifices. We beat and afflict our selves to pacify our Gods.
And when we be sick we use such ways to recover our health,
and to obtain all such things as we want, and desire to obtain
from our Gods.

PIUM.   Your prayers and powwowings are worshipping of the
Devil, and not of God, and they are among the greatest of your
sins. Your murders, lusts, stealing, lying, etc., they are great
sins. Your powwowings are worse sins, because by them you
worship the Devil instead of God. When you pauwaus use
physic by roots, and such other things which God hath made
for that purpose, that is no sin. You do well to use physic for

your recovery from sickness. But your praying to, and worshipping the Devil, that is your great sin, which now God calls
you to forsake. Use only such remedies as God hath appointed,
and pray to God.[26] This we call you to do, and this is the way
of true wisdom.

KINSMAN.   I feel my heart broken and divided. I know not what
to do. To part with our former lusts and pleasures is an hard
point and I feel my heart very loth and backward to it. Many
objections against it. I cannot but confess, that I do not in my
inward heart approve of them. I know they are vile and filthy,
and I desire to forsake them. They are like burning coals in my
bosom. I will shake them out if I can. I am ashamed of my old
ways, and loth I am to keep that which I am ashamed to be
seen in. The wiser men be, the more they abstain from such
lusts, and we account such to be foolish, vile and wicked, that
are unbridled and unpersuadable. I would not be myself of the
number of them that are vicious and vile above restraint. What
I persuade others to leave, I would not do the same myself.
We do account it commendable in such as do bridle and restrain
themselves from those vices, and what I judge to be commendable
in others, would be therein exemplar and a pattern unto such
as be young and foolish, and run mad after such beastly courses.
In that point I would easily be persuaded, or at least I desire
so to be. But the greatest difficulty that I yet find, is this. I am
loth to divide myself from my friends and kindred. If I should
change my course and not they, then I must leave and forsake
their company, which I am very loth to do. I love my sachem,
and all the rest of you my good friends. If I should change my
life and way, I greatly desire that we might agree to do it together.

SONT.   I like well that we should agree upon some amendment
of some bad courses that are too oft among us. And I love your
love that would have us agree together, and do what we do,
in these great matters, by common consent. But to do that is
a matter of much discourse, and deep consideration. This meeting was sudden. We have other matters at present to attend.
We have been together long enough for this time. We must
leave the whole matter to some other time.

PIUM.   Two days hence is the sabbath day. God hath commanded all men to *remember the sabbath day to keep it holy.* I request all of you to come together that day, and then I will further teach you (by the assistance of the Lord) touching this matter. And to persuade you to make this beginning to keep the sabbath, besides the commandment of the Lord, we have the reasons annexed by God himself unto it. God himself *rested that day*, to set us an heavenly pattern, and God hath also *blessed that day*, and made it holy, and hath promised that when we shall *meet together in his name, there he will come among us, and bring a blessing with him.* And when the disciples of Christ were met to worship God upon that day, before the day was done, he came among them and blessed them. So if you come together on the sabbath day, my hope and trust is, that we shall find some special token of the presence of Christ Jesus among us.[27]

KINSMAN.   I do very well like of this motion, and shall willingly attend. And if you think good, let my house be the place, or if you our beloved sachem think good, we will all come together at your house.

SONT.   I like it well. Let it be so. Come to my house, and you shall be welcome.

ALL.   Content, we like it well. So let it be.

PIUM.   Let the time of meeting be as early as you well can, about nine of the clock.

ALL.   So let it be.

THE SABBATH MEETING
SONTIM PIUM KINSMAN ALL

SONT.   It is well done my friends and neighbors, that you have remembered our agreement, and are come together about this great business. And now my kind friend, what have you further to say unto us? We are here ready to hear you.

PIUM. Six days God hath given us, wherein to do all our own business and works. Every seventh day God hath commanded us to give unto him, to rest from our own works, and to do his work, to pray unto him, to hear his word, to talk and speak of heavenly matters, for the good of our souls. We are all here this day before the Lord. And first of all he hath commanded us to pray together. Therefore let us all either stand up like servants, or kneel down like sons and daughters, and pray unto the Lord. Then he prayeth ——. The next work we use to do, is to catechize, that is, to teach by asking of questions, and they that are taught make answer according as they have been taught.[28] But that work you are not yet fitted and prepared for; therefore we lay it by. The next work which we do is to read some chapter of the word of God. *Then he calleth one that came with him, who readeth.* When that is finished, then he saith, now we used to sing a psalm, which is one part of God's word and worship. But for that work you are not yet prepared; therefore we lay that by also.

And now I will teach you out of the word of God. The text is Math. 7:13, 14. *Enter ye in at the strait gate, for wide is the gate, and broad is the way, that leadeth to destruction, and many there be which go in thereat. Because strait is the gate, and narrow is the way which leadeth unto life, and few there be that find it.*

In these words are two parts. 1. Here be two sorts of ways wherein men walk. 2. Here be two sorts of men that walk in these two ways. The first way is described by four things.

    1. There is a strait, little, narrow gate to enter in at.

    2. It is a narrow way, very rough, hard and difficult to walk in.

    3. Here is the end of this way whether it leadeth, viz. to heaven, happiness, glory and eternal life.

    4. Here be the numbers that get into, and walk in this way to get to heaven, *very few.*

The second way is described by four things.

    1. The gate of entrance is *broad* and *wide.*

2. The way itself is pleasant, easy, full of delights of the flesh, and of worldly pleasures.

3. Here is the end of this way. It leads to hell, to torments, and to eternal damnation.

4. Here be the numbers that walk in this way, *very many*. Most men in the world will choose to walk in this way, and at last go to hell torments.

The first sort of persons are good men and women, who

1. With much difficulty get into this way.

2. They patiently endure all difficulties in it.

3. They go to heaven and glory at last.

4. The number of them, they are but few.

The second sort of persons are wicked people, and these

1. Easily get into this way.

2. They take pleasure in it, and will not be persuaded to leave it, and get into the hard way.

3. The end of them all is, they go to hell torments.

4. The number of them, *a great many*. Most men are found in this way.

All these particulars he openeth, and insisteth upon, and concludeth with an exhortation.

1. To come out of this broad easy way, by considering the end of it, whither it leadeth.

2. To get into the hard way of praying to God, and patiently continue in it, considering the end it leads unto, even heaven and glory.

SONT.   What book is that you read in, and why do you call it *The Word of God?*

PIUM.   This is the book of God's law, which he hath taught holy men his prophets and apostles to write, and give unto us, to call us out of the broad way of sin and death, and to call us into the narrow way of repentence, faith in Jesus Christ, and eternal life.

SONT.   It may be the Englishmen made it, and tell you that they are the Words of God.

PIUM.   This book was written long before the Englishmen

prayed to God, and Englishmen have learned all their wisdom
out of this book. And now they have translated it for us, and
if we attend unto it, it will teach us wisdom, as it hath taught
them.

KINSMAN. You speak much of Jesus Christ, and his pardoning
our sins, and saving our souls. Who is this Jesus Christ?

PIUM. God is one in three, the Father, Son, and Holy Ghost.
Jesus Christ is God the Son, who became a man. And when
we deserved to die for our sins, he came and died for us. And
God hath promised that all that believe in Christ shall be pardoned of all their sins, and shall be glorified in heaven.

Touching this point I will teach in the afternoon.

THE AFTERNOON EXERCISE

PIUM. God requires we should give him a whole day, wherefor
it is not enough to worship God half a day. We are again come
together to worship God, and we shall do the same this afternoon, as we did in the forenoon. Let us pray.

After prayer, he taketh this text, Math. 1:21, 22, 23. This
text teacheth three things touching Jesus Christ.

1. His wonderful birth; *a virgin conceived.* Of which,
see Luke 1:26 to 39.

2. Two names; *John, Emmanuel.*

3. What Christ did for us, and doth, signified by his
name Jesus; He taketh away our sins. And this he doth two
ways. 1. He taketh away our sins out of God's sight, by dying
in our stead, and so meriting a pardon for all our sins. 2. He
taketh away our sins out of our own hearts, by working repentance in us, and faith in his name, giving us his spirit, and
sanctifying of us by his grace, and leading us to all holiness of
life and conversation.

The third part of this text is, how Jesus Christ is enabled to
do great things for us. This signified by his second name, *God
with us.*

Christ was God and man in one person, and that maketh his
death of infinite value with God, to obtain a pardon for all our
sins.

And this maketh him of infinite power to overcome our hearts, and turn them unto God.

These things are deep wisdom. Therefore pray unto God, and he will give you wisdom to understand them, James 1:5.

KINSMAN. I am amazed to hear these deep things. I am now more discouraged about praying to God. Alas, we cannot pray, nor read. How shall we keep a sabbath, and what shall we do?

PIUM. I will speak unto the church at Natick, and we shall send a wise man to teach you, to keep sabbaths among you, and all that I shall persuade you unto is to come together on the sabbaths, as you have done this day, and hear the Word of God, and then God will teach you.

KINSMAN. Oh that it might be so. I should gladly attend unto the word.

SONT. I say the same.

ALL. We like it well.

KINSMAN. I pray let it not be delayed.

PIUM. Lo, here is a manifest token of God's presence according to his promise. For who but God could bow all your hearts to hear the word of God, especially considering how averse you were at first. Now let us pray, and praise, and *give thanks to the God of heaven, for his mercy endureth forever.*[29]

Dialog. II
About Calling home poor INDIANS

Waban was sent forth upon the service of Christ unto sundry places, where passed such like discourses and acts.

WABAN[30]   PENEOVOT[31]

WABAN. Ho, well met friend. How far travel you this way?

PEN.   I am going to Nipmuk, a town which Nishohkou[32] is sachem. With him I have some business, which occasioneth my going thither.

WABAN.   Ha! You and I are both going alike in sundry things. I wish we might be both alike in one more thing. The things wherein we are alike are these; we are both tall men, we are met in the same way, we are going to the same place, our business is unto the same person, the sachem of the place.

PEN.   Ha, ha, he. I acknowledge what you say. But I pray what is that wherein you desire we might agree? For I do not understand that you have yet named that, and I the more desire to know that, because you do seem to put more weight upon that, than upon all the rest which you have named.

WABAN.   You judge right touching my opinion of that thing which I have not mentioned. But I doubt that you will not be of my mind if I should speak it, and for that reason I did conceal it. Wise men will cover and hide their jewels, and not expose them to everybody's sight, for they know some will lightly esteem them, because they know not their worth. But if they fall in company with such as know the worth of their jewel, they will be content to let them see it, and take a full view of it.

PEN.   Your discourse doth the more inflame my desire to know what this matter is that is so precious in your eyes, and so doubtful to find esteem with me. I confess I am foolish, but I hope you shall find me one that would be wise, and love the company of the wise, and willing to learn of others that wisdom which I want. And therefore though I desire not to know other men's secrets, yet if this other matter you intimate be such as I may know, my desire is raised high to know it.

WABAN.   Your words are good and wise, and give me hopes that what I have further to say unto you will find acceptance with you according to my desire. I will therefore open to you the truth of the matter. I am a *praying Indian.* I have left our old *Indian* customs, laws, fashions, lusts, pauwauings, and whatever else is contrary to the right knowledge of the true God, and of Jesus Christ our redeemer. It repenteth me of all my fore-past life, the lusts, vanities, pleasures, and carnal delights that were formerly very sweet and delightful to me, are now bitter as gall unto me. I hate and loathe them. All the works of darkness in which I was wont to take pleasure, I do now forsake and abandon. I am come into the light. I now see things as they are indeed, and not as they seemed to be in the dark. I now know the Word of God, which showeth me the way of eternal life. I now know God who made all the world, against whom mankind are turned rebels and sinners. I know the law of God which I have broken, and by my sins I have deserved eternal damnation in the world that is to come. I now know Jesus Christ, who hath died for us, to procure a pardon for us, and to open a door and way to eternal life and salvation for us. Into this way I have entered. Herein I walk, and I have promised to God, that I will live and walk in this way all the days of my life.

And not only so, but my desire is to persuade all others into the same way which I have entered, because I do certainly and experimentally know that my former ways were darkness, sin, and led unto hell and damnation. And this way wherein I am now entered is a way of light, life, holiness, peace, and eternal salvation. Therefore I do earnestly persuade all that I meet with to be wise, and turn from the ways of darkness, and come into this way of light and glory. And this is the thing which I did mean, when I said, *that there is another thing wherein I wish that we may be alike.* I do therefore exhort and entreat you that you would do as I have done. Forsake your old ways of sin, of which you have cause to be ashamed, and turn unto God, call on God, and be numbered among the *praying Indians.*

PEN. Oh I am surprised, I am amazed. You have ravished my soul. You have brought a light into my soul. I wonder at myself. Where have I been? What have I done? I am like one raised out of a dark pit. You have brought me forth into the sunshine. I begin to see about me. If I look back, and down into the pit where I have been all my days, I wonder at myself what dead

dark thing I have been. When I look upon you, I see you are
like an angel of light. I have heard of this business of praying
to God. Some have spoken ill of it. Some have spoken favorable. I could not tell what it was, but now by your discourse
I begin to see what an excellent thing it is. It changes men, and
advances them into a condition above other men. You have
dealt with me like as the fishers do by the fish. You laid a
bait for me to make me desire it, and bite at it. But I saw not
your hook, until you had catch'd my soul. And now I am
catch'd, I see it was not for my hurt, but for my great good.
The light which I do already see is a beautiful and desirable
thing, and therefore I pray you go on, and tell me more of
this new way.

WABAN.   The two first things you are to consider of now you
are come into the light, and your heart willing to attend unto
this great work of praying to God, are these:
    1. To know God
    2. Our selves
Of God, his greatness, goodness, wisdom, and power. He hath
made all things in this great world. All things above us are his
works. He made the heavens, the sun, moon, stars, clouds, etc.,
and all things below, the seas, the earth, and all things that are
in them. He made man, and gave him dominion over all his
works in this world, and a law of life, under the penalty of
damnation. And all this God did in six days, so great is God
above man. The law which he gave to man is holy, just and
good. But man by the temptation of evil angels, who by their
sin became to be devils, I say man broke the law which God
gave him, and sinned against God, turned rebel against God,
and served the Devil. And in this rebellion all the children of
men go on to this day.
    God's law is in ten commandments, wherein he requireth of
man to know and worship God, fear his name, and keep his
sabbath. And other laws forbid lust, murder, stealing, and all
other evils. Moreover, God hath annexed unto his law a great
promise, *do and live*, with a great punishment, *sin and die*
eternally. Namely, that all the breakers of this law, and sinners

against him, shall be punished in hell fire with eternal torments.
And this is the condition of all mankind, and it is our estate,
that by our sins against God we have deserved to die, and then
to be cast away down into hell fire, to be tormented among
the devils, who tempted us to sin, and whom we have served
in our life time. Now together with them we must be tormented
forever.

PEN.   Oh you have now killed me again. By the first light you
showed me, I thought you had made me alive, and I joyed in
the light. But I understood it not. Now your light is become a
sword. It hath pierced through my heart. By it I now see I am
a dead man. Alas, I have been a sinner all my days. I am guilty
of more sins than I have lived days. Many sins in a day have I
committed. Night and day have I offended God, and broke his
law. I have served the Devil and not God. I have done nothing
that God commandeth. I have only served the Devil, and committed sin. Therefore I have deserved to be damned in hell,
and to be tormented among the devils forever, whom in this
life I have served with so much delight. And now poor miserable
I, what shall I do? These trees under whose shade we sit, why
fall they not upon me and crush this rebellious worm to pieces,
and send me away to the place of eternal torment? These rocks
and hills about us, why fall they not upon me and break me
into dust and powder, and send me away unto perdition? Will
God regard these complaints of mine? What are these tears of
mine? Can they quench hell fire? Nay, will they not rather be
oil unto those flames? I am in misery, help I can find none. The
greatness of God's majesty and power, against whom I a finite
poor worm have sinned, doth most amaze me. I pray help me
further to understand the great majesty of God.

WABAN.   For this purpose this young man with us shall read
unto you some part of the word of God. Read the 40th chapter
of Isaiah, begin at the 12th verse, and read unto the 27th. *Who
hath measured the waters in the hollow of his hand, and meted
out heaven with a span, and comprehended the dust of the
earth in a measure, and weighed the mountains in scales, and*

the hills in a balance? etc. Again, read some chapters of Job, chapters 37, 38, 39, 40. When these chapters were read, Waban proceeded and said, Moreover, such is the omniscience and omnipresence of God, that we cannot hide from his sight any sin, or thought, nor yet can we hide our selves, or escape out of his hand. For this purpose read Psalm 139 verses 2, 10, 14. Thou knowest my downsitting, and uprising. Thou understandest my thoughts afar off, etc. Also God is unchangeable. For that read Mal. 3:6, For I am the Lord. I change not. Therefore ye sons of Jacob are not consumed. And without shedding of blood is no remission. Heb. 9:22.

PEN. Still I am more and more confounded. Who is able to deliver a wretched rebellious worm out of his almighty hand? Where shall I hide myself from his eye? Oh, that the rocks and mountains would fall upon me, and hide me from the stroke of his wrathful hand! And yet I see that my wish is vain. There is no escaping from his wrathful vengeance. Oh wretched I, what shall I do? Had I a word to give, I would freely give it, to be saved out of those flames, which are ready prepared for me, and I have so justly deserved. And yet I see that I have no such thing to give in ransom for my soul. Or had I such a thing to give, would it be accepted? God hath no need of my gifts or sacrifices. Oh what shall I do? My miserable soul must die.

WABAN. I am in the same condition with you, and so are we all. But I have rest and quiet in my soul, because I have found a ransom, with which God is well pleased. His wrath is pacified and I am delivered. I have escaped the danger of those deserved flames.

PEN. Your speeches are some stay to my distressed soul. It breedeth some hope in me to hear that there is a ransom to be found, and that you have found it. May there be hope that I also may find the same?

WABAN. Yea, there is hope in Israel touching this matter. It is as free for you as me.

PEN. Oh, that you would show me this remedy. You have shown me my misery and danger effectually. May it please the Lord to make you as successful to show me the remedy. But my soul is still drowned in doubt and fear. Oh how I long to hear where this remedy is to be found. I would go to the world's end to find it. I would take any pains to obtain it. But my trembling heart saith you and I both may be deceived. For what creature in all the world is able to deliver a soul from the hand of this omnipotent and all-seeing God, whose justice and law are unchangeable, and nothing save blood and death can satisfy it.

WABAN. True, no creature is able to deliver us. Vain is the help of man or angel in this case. As you said before, your mournings, cries, and tears cannot do it. None but God himself can do it, and your heart will say and yield that God himself can do it. Isaiah 55:9, as heaven is above earth, so are God's thoughts above ours.

PEN. Yea, that I can freely yield unto, that God himself can do it. What cannot he do? But will the offended just and holy God pacify himself for my offences, and pardon so great a sinner as I? God is just and holy, and how can it stand with his holy justice to pardon a vile sinner, without satisfaction to his holy justice? Will the holy God cease to be just? Will he abrogate and disannul his holy law, which I have so often, so deeply, so rebelliously broken? I have some hope, because you say it is so, but I see not yet how it can be, for God is unchangeable.

WABAN. It is true that you say God will never deny his own justice, nor abrogate his holy law for our sakes. But our God is a merciful God, and infinite in wisdom, and by his infinite wisdom he hath found out a way to satisfy the justice of his own law, and to deliver poor sinners from the condemnation of the law.

PEN. But how can that be? Can man, or any creature for him, satisfy the justice of the law of God? Oh I am in the dark about this matter. You speak of impossibilities.

WABAN.   Nothing that is holy, just, and good is impossible with God; and therefore to show you God hath done this, know, that God hath done it himself, and whatsoever God hath done is holy, just, and good.

PEN.   But I pray tell me how this can be? Oh how I long to hear of this way of deliverance of a poor sinner out of the hands of God's holy justice and unchangeable law.

WABAN.   I will (as well as I can) declare it unto you. God is one in three; Father, Son, and Holy Ghost: which we must believe and admire, though we cannot demonstrate. I shall at this time say no further of that point, only this much. God one in essence, in his infinite wisdom and understanding, conceiveth the image of himself as the only adequate object of his infinite wisdom. God conceiving is the Father. God conceived is the Son. This intellectual act of conceiving is called begetting. God conceiving, and God conceived, by an infinite act of volition, loveth himself, and this love is the Holy Ghost, proceeding from the Father and the Son. God as he is Father made all things, and giveth man a law. God in the dispensation of the covenant of works hath agreed within himself that the Son of God should assume unto himself an human nature, which is subject unto the law of God. This glorious person is God and man in one person, named Jesus Christ. This glorious person Jesus Christ, is a person of more worth than all mankind beside. This glorious person Jesus Christ came into this world, and offered to God by covenant his own life in our stead, and died for us to satisfy divine justice for the sin of man. With this sacrifice God hath said he is satisfied for the sin of man. Thus Jesus Christ hath honoured God's law, by satisfying of divine justice, and now Jesus Christ hath power to pardon whom he will.

PEN.   These are strange and deep things which you say. In this way I do see that a person is found that is able to pay a ransom to God, and satisfy his justice. But still I am in the dark about myself. How shall I be interested in this redemption wrought by Jesus Christ? If you have obtained it, I have some hope that so may I. I pray tell me how I may be made partaker of this great redemption from the condemnation of sin pronounced against me by the law of God.

WABAN.   According to my poor ability, as well as I can, I will tell you, and I will tell you how I have obtained it, and in the same way you also may obtain it.

PEN.   O how this hope, by your experience, beginneth to raise my heart. I pray go on and declare it to me.

WABAN.   God hath made a new covenant of grace which he hath opened in the gospel, and Jesus Christ hath published it to all the world. And the sum of it is this, that whosoever shall penitently turn from sin towards God, and believe in Jesus Christ, he shall have a pardon for all his sins, and be partaker of eternal life, through the grace and mercy of God in Jesus Christ. John 3:16, For God so loved the world, that he gave his only begotten son, that whosoever believeth in him should not perish, but have everlasting life.

PEN.   This puts me into another great difficulty. Can I penitently turn from sin, and believe in Jesus Christ? Alas, I know not how to go about such a work, much less do I know how to accomplish the same. Therefore I still am under great straits, and know not what to do.

WABAN.   You say true. It is a work past your ability to do. But Jesus Christ hath undertaken two great works in the salvation of sinners. 1. The first is to pacify God's justice, and satisfy the law, and to reconcile God toward us, and that he hath done and finished effectually, when he was here on earth. 2. Christ hath undertaken to conquer the world of all God's elect (for it is only the elect of God whom Christ hath undertaken for) and the Father and the Son have sent forth God the Holy Ghost to effect this work. For none but God himself is able to convert a soul, and create faith in the heart of man. We cannot do it of our selves, neither you nor I can do it, but by the assistance of the spirit of God, by the word of God.

PEN. Still the difficulty lieth before me. I am at a loss, and know not what to do. I fully believe I am not able to do it my self.

WABAN.   I will help you as well as I can, and the Lord will help you by his word and spirit. Your heart is now (in some measure) already turned away from sin. That part of the work is wrought in your heart, which I will demonstrate to you thus: I ask you, will you hereafter live and walk in the ways of sin as you have formerly done?

PEN. Oh no, no. I hope God will keep me and help me. I will never live again as I have formerly done. I will bind myself from it. I abhor to do so. I will forsake them forever. Lord help me so to do.

WABAN.   Well, therefore you are now converted from your sins. And who wrought this great change in you? It was not your self did it, nor was it I that did it. I only opened unto you the Word of God, but the spirit of God, by the conviction of the law, and by the Word of God, hath wrought this work in you.

PEN. I cannot gainsay you. I yield to what you say, and wonder at it.

WABAN.   In the same manner the spirit of God by the word is able to create faith in you to believe in Jesus Christ. This work the Lord useth to work in us by the promises of the gospel. Now I will propound unto you at present but one promise. Matthew 11:28, 29, Come unto me, all ye that labour and are heavy laden, and I will give you rest. Take my yoke upon you, learn of me; for I am meek and lowly in heart: and ye shall find rest unto your souls. Now I ask you, are you weary and heavy laden with your sins?

PEN. Oh yes, God knows I am so. I never felt the like distress in my soul since I was born. Sin is the bitterest thing in the world to my soul.

WABAN. Then hearken to this call of Christ, for he calls you in particular to come to him, and this coming is believing. Are you willing to come to Christ, and ask pardon of him, and beg his mercy?

PEN. Yea, with all my heart. Lord help me.

WABAN. Then see the next words, what he promises. I will give you rest.

PEN. Oh Lord let it be so, according to thy word and promise, thy will be done.

WABAN. Well, wait here, and see if God doth not quiet your soul, and give you rest. Meanwhile, I will farther ask you in the next words, are you willing to take upon you Christ his yoke, and this yoke consisteth of two parts. 1. The yoke of commandments, to do whatever he commandeth. And 2. His yoke of sufferings in this world for his name's sake. For now that you are converted, the carnal world will hate you, mock you, injure you, speak all evil against you, and it may be if they can they will kill you, as they did Christ. But are you willing to suffer all for Jesus Christ his sake, who hath died for you? And further, are you willing to learn meekness of Jesus Christ? For they are the next words, and I do assure you, that you will have great need of patience, when you have done all the duties he commands, to suffer patiently what God himself shall inflict upon you by sicknesses, crosses and temptations, or what wicked men shall inflict upon you.

PEN. These things which you speak are against the flesh and frame that I used to be in. And I do find that they are not so

fully killed, but that they have a little stirring in them when
you propound these cases to me.

But the experience I have now found of the love of God,
and of Jesus Christ to my soul, doth lay such an engagement
upon my heart, that I will, by his grace and assistance, be for
him only, serve him only, do all that ever he shall command
me, suffer whatever he shall impose upon me. I will no more
be for myself, but for him, who hath done all this for me. Oh
what shall I render unto the Lord for all his benefits to my
poor soul!

WABAN. We are surprised by the night. We must rest under
these trees this night. I do account this day well spent, though
we have made but little progress toward the place of our intent-
ment. But I have been about the work I came abroad upon,
though not the persons I intended. Thus God doth over rule the
ways of men. He foreseeth and ordereth that which we had no
thoughts upon. And therefore in that we have spent this day
in such conference and discourse, wherein we have seen so much
of the presence of Christ with us, let us now spend this night
in prayers and praises unto the Lord, who hath found us before
we sought for him. You were going about another business.
You little thought of finding Jesus Christ by the way, and finding mercy to your soul, a pardon of your sins, and to become a
praying Indian.

PEN. Your discourse doth heighten my admiration. I acknowledge God hath thought of me when I thought not of him. He
had a care of my soul when I had no care of myself. God hath
plucked me out of darkness, and brought me into a most wonderful light, that I should be forced to see the wonderful things of
God's law, and of my eternal condemnation by it, my helpless
and hopeless condition that I was in.

And then, that the Lord should open unto me a possibility
of escape, that a ransom and remedy might be found by the
infinite wisdom and mercy of God. And that Jesus Christ had
not only accomplished that great work, but offered the fruit
and benefit of it to me, and called me to rest in him, and to
betrust my soul with him for pardon of all my sins, and for

eternal life in Jesus Christ. These things are matter of my admiration, and shall be to all eternity. My life remaining shall be
spent in admiring and in obeying and suffering, as you have now
taught me. I shall account nothing too dear of Christ, who hath
not accounted his own most precious life too dear for me.
Whereas I am now instructed, that he being God and man in
one person, his life was of more value than all the lives of all
mankind; and that he did not forbear to offer that precious
life for me; I must, I will, by his grace assisting, admire at this
mercy forever. And therefore the motion that you made of
spending the night in prayer and praises to his holy name, it is
the most acceptable motion to my heart. My experience sug-
gesteth unto me matter abundantly to pray and praise his name.
But my ignorance is such as that I cannot tell how to utter my
mind in words of knowledge suitable unto so great mercies as
I have now experienced.

WABAN.   Your discourse doth lead me out to inform you in a
great point of the grace and kingdom of Jesus Christ, and that
is the gift and grace of prayer, which the spirit of Jesus Christ
teacheth every new born soul to perform. For so the scripture
saith, Rom. 8:15, *He hath given the spirit of his son, whereby
we cry.* And crying is an earnest manner of praying. And the
matter of our cry is to say *Abba, Father,* that is, to call God
our father, and to ask him a child's portion in the name of
Jesus Christ, as he hath promised, that whatever we ask in the
name of Jesus Christ, it shall be surely granted, either the same
thing or better. For we are foolish children, and know not what
is best for our selves, but the father doth. And therefore when
we make our prayers and request unto God, we must leave the
matter to his love and wisdom, to give us what, and when, and
how he will.

And because we are ignorant what to pray for, therefore
the spirit of God who dwelleth in our heart, he is called the
spirit of grace and supplication; and Rom. 8:26, 27, Likewise
the Spirit also helpeth our infirmities: for we know not what
we should pray for as we ought: but the Spirit itself maketh
intercession for us with groanings which cannot be uttered.
And he that searcheth the hearts knoweth what is the mind of

the Spirit, because he maketh intercession for the saints according to the will of God. Here we see that our weakness is supplied by the assistance of the spirit, and he helpeth us to pray for such things as please God, and in such a manner as pleaseth God. And this is the condition of every true converted believer, that he can pray, and desires to pray, and is ever lifting up his heart to God in prayer. And therefore I like it well that my motion of spending this night in prayer is so acceptable to you. A good sign it is that the spirit of Jesus Christ hath taken possession of your soul.

PEN.   This little sight and experience I have hath so filled my heart with a sense of my own vileness, that I see matter of endless confession. And I see so much nothingness in my self that I see endless matter of petition and supplication. And I see my self infinitely obliged to God for the riches of his free grace to me a rebellious worm, that I see infinite matter of praise, thanksgiving and admiration. My heart also longeth after others, that they may be as I am. I pray tell me, what is my duty in that respect to pray for others, my relations, my friends, my neighbors, and for all?

WABAN.   Christ hath taught us, *when thou are converted, then strengthen thy brother*, Luke 22:32. Therefore you must pray for all the church of God. You must especially pray for them that are weak, and tempted, and afflicted. And you must pray for them that are not yet converted, and for all God's people, and for all God's cause in the world, and for the fulfilling of all God's promises. There is a world of matter to pray for, and for Kings and rulers in a special manner.

PEN.   I feel your heart to answer your words like an echo. My heart answers, all these things I desire to pray for. But alas, I am ignorant of fit words in prayer, and therefore I do request of you, first do you pray, and set me a pattern. [Waban prayeth]

PEN.   Many nights I have spent waking, sometime in hunting, sometime worse, in dancing and other sinful revels. But I never spent a night so well in my life before. It is the first night of my new life. I have begun to live well. Oh how full of fear, and care and desire my heart is, that I may go on according to this good beginning. I hope the sweet savour of this good beginning to live well shall abide with me, and I desire your help and counsel how I may so perform it.

WABAN.　　Our state in this world is not perfect. Corruption is killed but in part. There be old roots remaining, which upon occasion offered will still be stirring, acting, appearing, as a tree that is cut down, the old roots will be growing, which must be kept down with a speedy cutting off. A field that is well weeded will quickly produce new weeds again, out of that natural propensity of the earth to bring forth weeds. But a watchful and diligent husbandman will be often weeding over his corn fields. And so will our hearts be sending forth new weeds of sin, but we must be daily diligent to watch and weed them out. Our hearts have a natural propensity to sin, and therefore must be kept with all diligence. And therefore that is the first counsel that I give you, out of the experience of my own naughty heart.

PEN.　　Your words do put a fear into my heart. I know that old customs of sin are very hardly left, and I have been so long accustomed to sin, that I am afraid of my self.

WABAN.　　Fear is a good watchman; *happy is the man that feareth always.* [33] And let this put you on to a second counsel that I give you. Be much and often in prayer, and that not only among others in family worship, and public worship, but also, and most frequently in secret prayer. For so Christ hath commanded, Math. 6, and Christ himself hath set us an example, who spent whole nights in prayer.

PEN.　　The night spent in prayer hath let me find a sweet taste in it, though I do already find that it is a weariness to my flesh. I thank you for this counsel. I desire I may remember and do it. What further counsel will you give me?

WABAN.　　You must be much conversant in the Word of God,

and though you cannot yet read the word, yet you must get
the help of others, and learn the Word of God by heart. And
you must meditate upon the same night and day, for so David
did, Psalm 1:2. And the meditation on the word will sanctify
the heart, and kill corruption, and will mightily help you to
subdue it.

PEN.   I doubt it will be difficult for me to learn to read. I am
full of capacity.

WABAN.   A strong desire, diligence and constancy, will obtain
any thing, and you must pray God to teach you, and to open
your heart to learn: James 1:5, If any of you lack wisdom, let
him ask of God, that giveth to all men liberally, and upbraideth
not; and it shall be given him. And for a further help to you,
my fourth counsel is, that you diligently learn the catechism,
and by learning to read that, you will learn to read and understand the whole Bible.

PEN.   I see myself very ignorant, and therefore I am very desirous to learn catechism, because I have heard and do perceive
that is the foundation of all knowledge in religion, being wisely
gathered out of the scripture.

WABAN.   You say right about catechism. We do therefore teach
it to our children, that the principles of good knowledge may be
sown and rooted in them from a child. And for that reason also
do we send them to school, to learn to read the Word of God,
that they may be acquainted with the word from a child.

PEN.   Oh what a loss this is to me, that I am to begin to learn
catechism and the Word of God now I am a man, which I might
have been acquainted with from a child, had I been brought up
among the *praying Indians.* How happy are your children that
are thus brought up. I suppose you are very diligent in this
matter in training up of your children.

WABAN.   We have great cause to judge ourselves for too much
negligence in this point. A fifth counsel I give you is, that you

be constant and diligent in the exercise of the worship of God
in your family, in these points: 1. You must morning and
evening pray in your family, and teach them in catechism,
and reading of the scriptures. 2. Always before and after meat
you must pray and give thanks to God.

PEN.   Oh what an holy life do the praying Indians live. Lord
teach me and help me thus to do. What further counsel do you
give me?

WABAN.   A sixth counsel I give you is, that you do carefully
remember the sabbath day to keep it holy, and to come to the
public assembly both forenoon and afternoon, constantly and
timely, and there diligently to attend the worship of God.

PEN.   Oh how my heart approveth of this counsel. Have you
any further counsel to give me?

WABAN.   One thing more. Let all your conversation be a good
example to others, and labor on all occasions to do good to
others.

PEN.   I request this of you. That as we travel this day in our
journey, you would teach me the principles of catechism.

WABAN.   I do well like of your motion. It's a good subject of
discourse as we are in our way.

Thus they are employed till they come to their journeys end.

WABAN   NISHOHKOU   PENEOVOT

WABAN.   My aged uncle, I am glad that it hath pleased God
once more to give me an opportunity to see you alive in this
world. It is not unknown unto you, that I and many others
have undertaken a new way of life, which is known to many

by the name of *Praying to God*. The way that I formerly, and
you still live in, is a way of worshipping the Devil. It is a way
of darkness and sin. And though it is a way pleasant and easy
to the flesh, yet it leadeth to destruction and eternal torments.
Man is made for another life after this life is ended. And though
our body dieth and turneth to dust, yet the soul is immortal.
It dieth not, but at the death of the body it departeth to a
place of eternal being, either in glory, or in misery. If we pray
to God with a right heart, penitently from sin to God, and believe in Jesus Christ, then we shall have a pardon granted us,
and eternal happiness with Jesus Christ. But if we do not turn
to God, but worship and serve the Devil, and walk in the ways
of sin, then at death our soul must be dragged to hell, and there
tormented forever among the devils, whom we have obeyed
and served in this life. These things, and many more, do we
perfectly know, and believe to be true by the word of God,
which is the sunlight of the soul, even as the sun is the great
light of the outward world.

God hath put it into my heart to desire that your soul might
be blessed forever. And the church hath sent me, and I come
in the name of Jesus Christ to tell you these things, and beseech you to turn from these vain and evil ways, and to believe
in Jesus Christ, that your sins may be pardoned, and that your
soul may be saved in eternal glory.

NISH.   Your love and desire of my good, I have no reason but
to accept with kindness. But me thinks one thing in your discourse is doubtful. We see with our eyes, and know certainly
that the body dieth, and turneth to rottenness and dust, and
why may not the soul do so likewise? We see not what becom-
eth of it, and to make such a stir, and change our course upon
uncertainties, I have no liking of it. My age inclineth me rather
to be quiet, and not meddle with such unseen intricacies, fitter
for younger heads to mind.

WABAN.   Our bodies are the product of the seed of man, and
that is made out of the food we eat, and our food grows out of
the earth, so that our bodies are made of refined earth. And
therefore at death turn to earth again, out of which it was

made. And so God speaketh, *dust thou art, and unto dust thou shalt return.*[34] But the soul is not so. It is a spirit, of a purer nature than earthly things, and immediately created by God, and therefore dieth not. Besides, we are assured by many infallible proofs out of the word of God, and by evidence of good reason, that the soul is immortal, which point we are taught in our catechism. And not only so, but God hath taught us, that at the end of the world the body shall be raised again out of the dust, and the soul and body joined together again, and then the person shall be judged by Jesus Christ, according to their deeds done in the flesh. Those that live and die in their sins shall be turned into hell, to be tormented by and with the devils. But they that turn to God, and believe in Jesus Christ, shall be judged to go with Christ to heaven and be ever with him in eternal glory.

Therefore this consideration doth more sharpen my request and entreaties of you. How shall I endure to see this body of yours, which I so respect and love, and that soul of yours also, to go away unto eternal torments. And I pray you consider what a wound and torment it will then be, to remember, I was exhorted and entreated to turn to God and live. Mercy in Christ was offered me, but I refused it. And therefore deservedly do you lose what you refused, and deservedly you suffer that torment you did choose, rather than to trouble your self with this business of praying to God, and believing in Jesus Christ.

NISH. These are great and deep things that I understand not. You young men have your blood warm, and your wits fresh and ripe. You can read and understand these things. I am old and cold and dry, and half dead already. I have not strength enough left to be whetted up to such a new edge. Let me alone to die in quiet. Why should I take upon me such a disquiet to my mind, and disturbance to my self, and to my people? I have two sons young and active men. I am very willing that they should take up this new way. Persuade them to it if you will. But as for me, I am too old for such an undertaking.

WABAN. You do well to permit your sons to enter into the way of wisdom, and pray unto God. But I would propose two requirements unto you. 1. To do well for yourself as well as for your sons, for your own soul is as precious as their souls be. And 2. The most effectual means to persuade your sons unto this way of wisdom, is for you to set them an example. If you should choose this way, then it is like that they would follow your example. But if you refuse it yourself, there is the less hope that they will choose it. For it is a way hard to the flesh, and requires much subduing of lusts, which will rather be done in your decrepit age, than by them in their flourishing youth.

NISH.   I am weary, and need some food, and it is like so do you after your travel. And here is meat set before us. Therefore I pray eat, and you are welcome.

WABAN.   I pray you let us eat like praying Indians. God hath taught us that always when we eat we should pray and give thanks to God.

NISH.   I pray do so. It pleaseth me well, though I cannot do so myself, for I am ignorant of the ways of praying to God.

WABAN.   [Prayeth for a blessing, and then they eat. And after meat doth the same again.]

PEN.   Aged sachem, now that you and we are refreshed and strengthened by this food, I will declare unto you strange news, to which I entreat your attendance a little while, and all the people here present. I am like a man that was looking for a shell, and found a pearl of inestimable value, whereby he became very rich and renowned. I had a small occasion to come and visit you, grave sachem, and by the way I met with this good man, a messenger of God, by whose discourse my blind eyes are opened, my dead heart is made alive, my lame legs are enabled to walk in the way to heaven, where I shall enjoy an eternal kingdom. Many miracles have been wrought upon me by the power of God's word, spoken to me by this man. And that I may stir up your heart, and the hearts of the people here present to give diligent heed to what he saith, I will declare unto you what passed between us. I was as you are. I lived as

you live. I did as you do, and as the rest of our countrymen
and neighbors do. I followed the sports, pleasures, vanities, and
courses that other men, and you, to this day walk in. But I was
not aware how blind, and dead, and vile, and wicked I was in
the sight of God. Nor was I aware that I was running on in a
pleasant delightful way, which led me down to hell and eternal
damnation.

But when I met this man, he discoursed with me about these
things. He opened unto me, by the Word of God, the great
majesty of God, his holiness, justice, and goodness; how God
had made this great world, and all things in it, both things above,
and things below; how he made man an eminent creature, gave
him dominion over all the creatures here below, and gave him
an holy, just and good law, in Ten Commandments, under the
order of a covenant of works, and if he kept and obeyed this
law, he should live in glory and happiness forever. But if he did
break this law, and sin against God, that great majesty of heaven,
then he should be answerably and justly punished with eternal
torments in hell fire, with the Devil and his angels for evermore.
And this law was for himself and all his posterity, in whose
stead he stood as a public person.

Now he informed me, that Adam the first man sinned by the
temptation of evil angels, which rebelled against God, and turned
devils. By their temptation Adam sinned, and turned rebel
against God, and served, believed, and obeyed the Devil. And
therefore by the law of God he was judged and condemned,
and all his posterity. All this I found to be true in my own experience, for I went on in the same rebellion, breaking the holy
law of God every day both in thought, word, and deed, obeying
the Devil and his temptations, serving the lusts of my flesh, and
filthy mind. I walked in the broad, easy, pleasant way that
leadeth to destruction, so that I have deserved to be damned a
thousand, thousand times. And the greatness of the majesty of
God against whom I sinned, did breed terror in my soul. My
just condemnation by the law of God was evident to me as the
light. God's pure and unchangeable justice, which sentenced me
by the law unto hell, I saw I could not possibly answer, seeing
I am a poor finite worm. And what have I to satisfy infinite

offended justice? And therefore my soul mourned and lamented, and sunk into despair. For God's justice is unchangeable, and his law must be satisfied, which I am never able to do, and therefore I must be eternally damned under that just sentence. I durst not pray God to pardon my transgression, by any absolute sovereign act of mercy, for then he should have offended his own justice, which is unchangeable, and abolished his own law, whose perfection is such that it must be fulfilled and satisfied; and to satisfy God; was not in the power of any finite creature, man or angel. And therefore I despaired. No ransom could be found in all the world for me a poor sinner. Oh the bitterness that my soul felt. I had a taste of hell torments in my soul. My meditation of God's omniscience, whereby he knew all my sins, not only open, but secret ones, brought innumerable sins to my remembrance, one of which was enough to damn me. But I had mountains of guilt heaped upon my distressed soul. The impossibility for me to satisfy divine justice, and the impossibility of pardon without satisfaction, because God cannot be unjust, and his law is unchangeable. Such meditations cast me into the horrible pit of darkness and desperation. *The redemption of their soul is precious, and it ceaseth forever.* Psalm 49:8.

Then God opened the mouth of this dear servant of his, who told me that the infinite mercy and wisdom of God had found out a ransom, a way to satisfy justice, and fulfill the law, and to save poor condemned sinners, and that he himself had found mercy in that way. This bred some hope in my soul, and stayed me from sinking quite down, when I heard of a possibility. But still I was in distressing doubt and fear that it was but some delusion, because I could not see a possibility for man or angel, nor any creature, to satisfy and give a ransom to infinite justice.

Then he declared to me, that it is true that no creature could give a ransom to satisfy justice, but God himself was able to satisfy the infinite justice of God. To that I yielded, that God himself might satisfy his justice. But still I was in the dark. I could not see this could possibly be. Then he opened to me that adored doctrine of God, his being one and three, how God was one in essence, three in persons, God the Father, God the

Son, and God the Holy Ghost; how the Father doth by an
eternal intellectual act conceive the image of himself, as being
the only adequate object he understands himself; and this is
called the beginning of the Son, by an intellectual conception
of his own image. And these two subsistencies do by an eternal
act of volition love each other, and this love is the third person
in trinity, proceeding from both the Father and the Son.

Now the eternal majesty of God agreed with himself, that
God the Son, the second person in trinity, should assume human
nature to himself, and become a man, subject to the law. This
glorious person was the greatest subject that ever the law had,
and this glorious person is able perfectly to fulfill the law,
and perfectly to pay a ransom satisfactory to infinite justice,
who hath done it. This depth of divine wisdom my soul admired,
and shall do to eternity.

But still I was at a loss how I should be interested in the ransom that this glorious person hath paid. Then did this messenger
of God declare unto me, that this glorious person Jesus Christ
had undertaken both parts of this work: first to atone, and
reconcile God to man, by paying the ransom required, and by
perfect fulfilling the law: secondly, to subdue the soul and will
of man to turn and submit to be reconciled to God. But this
work of converting a soul to God is such, that as no man can
convert himself, so no other creature is able to do it. Only God
himself can do it. And for that end, both the Father and the
Son have sent forth the Holy Ghost, the eternal spirit, to work
upon the hearts of men, and to create the work of faith in
them by the word, and then to take possession of, and dwell in
believing souls, to mortify their lusts, to sanctify their hearts
and lives, and to lead them in the way of grace unto glory.

And further he declared unto me, that this blessed spirit of
God, by the Word of God, had already begun this great work in
my soul. For a new light is set up in my soul, a work beyond
the reach of man. And that light hath convinced me of sin, and
of my damned estate by sin. It had made a separation and divorce betwixt sin and my soul. It had cut me off the old stock,
and laid my soul down at the foot of Christ, capable with all
humble thankfulness to accept salvation, not by any merit of
mine, but by free grace of Christ unto a vile and unworthy

sinner. This I could not deny, but I did find such conviction, and such a submission to Christ. And this he declared to be the first step and beginning of the work of sound conversion.

I crave your patience a few words more. Then he proceedeth to show me that the work was finished by the promise, which also the spirit of God doth bring home unto the soul, and makes up the match betwixt Christ and the soul. And to that purpose he brought Math. 11:28, 29, by which text he showed me, as in a glass,

1. The distress my soul was in.
2. The call of Christ to such distressed soul.
3. The promise of rest to such as come to him.
4. The obligation to learn meekness, both to do and suffer the will of Christ. And here my soul resteth.

Ah, friends, we poor Indians are great sinners. But Christ is great salvation for the greatest sinners. What finite creature can outsin infinite satisfaction?

NISH.   I see you are strongly changed and transported. But my feeble age needeth rest, and so may you also by this time.

WABAN.   Aged uncle, tomorrow is the sabbath day. If you like of it, order all your people to come together in the morning, and by the Lord's assistance I will further teach you by the Word of God.

NISH.   I like it well. Send out to all parts of the town, that all meet tomorrow morning.

THE SABBATH   MANY BEING MET

WABAN.   The Lord hath appointed that in our public worship *first of all, supplications, intercessions, and giving of thanks be made for all men: for kings, and for all that are in authority, that we may lead a quiet and peaceable life in all godliness and honesty. For this is good and acceptable in the sight of God*

*our Savior: Who will have all men to be saved, and to come
unto the knowledge of the truth*, I Timothy 2:1-4. According
to this appointment, let us pray. Which finished, he took that
text, Matthew 20:1-7. In these words we may observe these
things:

1. The *vineyard* where men labour, is the church, and
this way of praying to God. And showeth that it is a laborious
and a good work, and will cause us to bring forth good fruits,
grapes and wine, which is pleasing to God and man. But beware
of bringing forth sour grapes. Especially suffer no briars and
thorns, but cut them down, and root them up, and cast them
out.

2. The *Lord of this vineyard* is Jesus Christ, who calleth
all men to come into this his vineyard, and do these works. And
this day I do in the name of the Lord Jesus Christ call you all
to pray to God, to come and work in this vineyard. Harken to
this call, and be no longer idle. Follow your sins no longer.
You have lived in sin long enough. Stay no longer, but come
in when you are called. Happy are you, if you obey and come.
Woe be to you, if you refuse.

3. Here be the several seasons of men's coming in, or
the several ages of men that do come in. 1. Some come in while
it is morning, that is, while they be young. Therefore I call you
boys, youths and girls, come you unto the Lord's vineyard,
and give unto God the first fruits of your days. 2. The Lord
went forth at the third hour, and called in young men and
young women to the call of God, and come in. 3. The Lord
went forth at the ninth hour, that is, he called in men and
women full grown, to ripeness of parts, and strength. You are
called this day to come into the Lord's vineyard. Be you persuaded to come in, and serve the Devil no longer. Now turn
unto the Lord. 4. The Lord went forth the eleventh hour, that
is, a little before night. And this doth mean you old men, and
old women, come you into the Lord's vineyard. You see the
Lord will accept you if you come. Do not think you are too
old to serve the Lord. If your days be near finished, you had
the more need to come in quickly, lest you die in your sins,
and perish forever.

When he had finished, an objection was made by one. *We*

dare not come in to pray to God, for we hear you are very
severe if any be found in sin, of lust or the like, you whip them
and punish them. That maketh us afraid to pray to God.

Answer. *WABAN.* God hath appointed punishments of sin to
be physic for their souls. And though physic be bitter and
sharp, yet it is very wholesome, good and needful. If you were
invited to dwell at such a town where there is a physician,
would you say, No, I will not dwell there, because if I be sick
I must take physic? Sure you would therefore go dwell at that
place. So it is in this case. You should therefore desire to pray
to God, because they use physic to heal the sickness of your
souls.

AFTERNOON   THEY BEING MET,

Waban having first prayed, then taketh this text, Psalm 2:8-11.
In these words see these three things.

    1. Christ Jesus taketh possession of the heathen, and
utmost ends of the earth: and this is one description of our
country. And now Jesus Christ calleth us to come to him. Some
of us have submitted unto Christ, and he hath mercifully accepted us, and so he will accept you, if you will come in unto
him.

    2. See what Christ will do to them that will not come
in. *He will break them with a rod of iron, and dash them in*
pieces like a potter's vessel. [35] Thus Christ will deal with our
sins, if we submit to him. But if we will not submit to him, he
will thus deal with our persons, and destroy them that refuse
to serve him, Luke 19:27.

    3. Here is the effect of God's severity against sinners.
Be wise therefore oh you kings; be instructed ye judges of the
earth: Serve the Lord with fear, and rejoice with trembling. [36]
Do not say, because Christ is severe against our sins, therefore
we will not come unto him, but fly from him. Do not so, for
then he will destroy you. But come trembling to him, and say,
Lord take away our sins by sharpness, that our souls may be
saved forever.

Dialog. III

Anthony[37] and William Abahton[38] were sent to Paganoehket,[39] where Philip is Sachem.
When they first came to the town, they went to the sachem's house.

ANTHONY   WILLIAM   PHILIP KEITASSCOT[40]   ALL THE COMPANY

ANTHONY.   Sachem, we salute you in the Lord, and we declare unto you, that we are sent by the church, in the name of our Lord Jesus Christ, to call you, and beseech you to turn from your vain conversation unto God, to pray unto God, and to believe in Jesus Christ for the pardon of your sins, and for the salvation of your soul. We do unto you, according to the holy example which we find, John 1:40-47, where Andrew called Peter, and Christ himself called Philip, and Philip called Nathaniel. So we are come this day unto you, in the name of Jesus Christ, to call you to come unto the Lord, and serve him. This argument we persuade you by, because we hear that many of your people do desire to pray to God, only they depend on you. We pray you to consider that your love to your people should oblige you to do them all the good you can. In this point, it lieth in your hand to do the greatest good in the world unto them, to do good to their souls as well as their bodies, and to do them good to eternity, as well as in this present world. All this good you will do to your people if you will accept of this offer of mercy. You will not only yourself turn from sin unto God, to serve the true and living God, but all your people will turn to God with you, so that you may say unto the Lord, oh Lord Jesus, behold here am I, and all the people which thou hast given me. We all come unto thy service, and promise to pray unto God so long as we live. Oh how welcome will you be unto the Lord? And oh how happy and joyful will all your people be, when they and their sachem are all owned by God, to be in the number of his children and servants. It will be a joy to all the English magistrates, and ministers, and churches, and good people of the land, to hear that Philip and all his people are turned to God, and become praying Indians. We read in Luke 15:7 that there is joy in heaven over one poor sinner that repenteth and turneth unto God. What great joy will it then be in heaven when so great a number as you and your people be, are turned unto the Lord and become praying Indians!

KEIT.   Often have I heard of this great matter of praying unto God, and hitherto I have refused. Mr. Eliot, Junior,[41] while he was alive, attempted it, but I did not hearken unto his persuasion. Old Mr. Eliot himself did come unto me. He was in this town, and did persuade me. But we were then in our sports, wherein I have much delighted, and in that temptation, I confess, I did neglect and despise the offer, and lost that opportunity. Since that time God hath afflicted and chastised me, and my heart doth begin to break. And I have some serious thoughts of accepting the offer, and turning to God, to become a praying Indian, I myself and all my people. But I have some great objections, which I cannot tell how to get over, which are still like great rocks in my way, over which I cannot climb. And if I should, I fear I shall fall down the precipice on the further side, and be spoiled and undone. By venturing to climb, I shall catch a deadly fall to me and my posterity.

The first objection that I have is this, because you praying Indians do reject your sachems, and refuse to pay them tribute, in so much that if any of my people turn to pray unto God, I do reckon that I have lost him. He will no longer own me for his sachem, nor pay me any tribute. And hence it will come to pass, that if I should pray to God, and all my people with me, I must become as a common man among them, and so lose all my power and authority over them. This is such a temptation as no other I, nor any of the great sachems, can tell how to get over. Were this temptation removed, the way would be more easy and open for me to turn praying Indian. I begin to have some good likance of the way, but I am loth to buy it at so dear a rate.

WILLIAM.   Though I am younger than my brother with whom I am sent, yet I know myself to be in a clear capacity to answer to this case, than my brother is, because Cutshamoquin,[42] the first great sachem that prayed to God, and after his death Chikautabuk,[43] and after him Misquamug,[44] were sachems in the town where I live, and they were my sachems, and I well know how the praying Indians did carry the matter towards them.

And first, I say, if any of the praying Indians should be disobedient (in lawful things) and refuse to pay tribute unto their sachems, it is not their religion and praying to God that teaches them so to do, but their corruptions. It is a sickness that needeth physic to cure it, and not allowance and countenance to defend it. I am sure the word of God commandeth all to be subject to the higher powers, and to pay them tribute, Romans 13:1-7. And Christ Jesus hath commanded to give unto Caesar the things that belong to Caesar, and to God the things that belong to God. And thus we have been taught. All the time that Cutshamoquin lived, our town did always honor, obey and pay tribute unto him, and so far as I know, so did all the praying Indians which belonged to his jurisdiction. After his decease we chose Josias or Chikautabuk, but not until he had promised before the Governor and Magistrates of the Massachusetts at Boston, to pray unto God, and to defend and govern us in praying to God all the days of his life. And though he fell back from his promise, yet our town always owned him. And when he began to recover himself a little before his death, the people were ready to adhere unto him, and acknowledge him. In his lifetime we accepted his brother, at his request; and Misquamug his leaving us, in his own act and not ours. And therefore, beloved sachem, let not your heart fear that praying to God will alienate your people from you. Nay, be assured it will more firmly oblige their hearts unto you. This I know by experience, for the more beneficent you are unto them, the more obligation you lay upon them. And what greater beneficence can you do unto them than to further them in religion, whereby they may be converted, pardoned, sanctified, and saved?

ANTHONY.   All that my brother hath said I second, and can bear witness unto. Only I will add one thing more of which I know more than he doth, because it was acted in the town where I live. There was some subtle endeavor to have mingled the praying and non-praying Indians, and to have reduced the praying Indians under the power of non-praying Indians, contrary to public and evident condition. Against this did some of the wiser sort (who saw the trap) firmly stand, giving this reason: the fox came to the lamb's door, and would fain come in, but the lambs refused. Then the fox desired to let him put in but one claw. The lambs refused, saying, if he get in but one claw, he will not rest till he have wriggled in his whole body. Stop waters while they are small and superable. And this I say unto you, beloved sachem, you shall find none truer to you than praying Indians. But know withall, that God teaches them by his word to be wise, and they will not easily be abused.

KEIT.   If that be true which you say, all is not true that is talked against the praying Indians. And indeed I do see that they are the worser sort of men that do speak so ill of them. The wiser sort are not so minded. I have nothing within the compass of my knowledge to gainsay that which you have spoken, and I know not but that a course may be taken to oblige both sides, as you took a course to oblige your sachem. I am ready to think that the Governor and Magistrates of the Massachusetts would as well oblige you to him, as him to you.

ANTHONY.   Yea, yea, so it was, and most equal that it should be so.

KEIT.   I have another objection stronger than this, and that is, if I pray to God, then all my men that are willing to pray to God will (as you say) stick to me, and be true to me. But all such as love not and care not to pray to God, especially such as hate praying to God, all these will forsake me, yea will go and adjoin themselves unto other sachems that pray not to God. And so it will come to pass, that if I be a praying sachem, I shall be a poor and weak one, and easily be trod upon by others, who are like to be more potent and numerous. And by this means my tribute will be small, and my people few, and I shall be a great loser by praying to God. In the way I am now, I am full and potent, but if I change my way and pray to God, I shall be empty and weak.

ANTHONY.   I confess that this is a strong temptation, and requireth much self-denial and faith to conflict with it. I pray consider what counsel Jesus Christ giveth in this case, Matthew 16:25, Let a man deny himself, take up his cross, and follow me. I confess that this is harsh doctrine to flesh and blood, but I will tell you a cordial against it, Matthew 19:29, And every one that hath forsaken houses, or brethren, or sisters, or father, or mother, or wife, or children, or lands, for my name's sake, shall receive an hundredfold, and shall inherit everlasting life. Trust God in this promise, and see if he do not perform it. And be assured, it is better to trust God in a way of well doing, than to trust to wicked and vile men in a way of sin. If God will punish you, all your men, especially the worst of them, cannot save you. But if all your men should forsake you, and yet you choose Christ, and be true to him, then Christ will certainly take care of you. And further, this is but a fear that human reason maketh. Try the Lord. It may be he will make all your men to stick the closer to you. You think the better sort will stick to you, it is but the loss of the worser sort, at the worst. And if you trust in the Lord, he can overrule the hearts of the worst of men, and they shall not forsake you. Besides, you may put it to the trial, put it to the public vote. If you should do so, I do think that they will all promise to stick unto you if you pray to God. And then this objection is cut off at the beginning of the work. Consider also what Christ hath said, Matthew 11:29-30, he commands such as come to him, to take up my yoke, and learn of me, for I am meek and lowly of heart, and you shall find rest to your souls: for my yoke is easy, and my burden is light. You fear that this will be burdensome, heavy, and to your loss. Try the Lord if he do not make this objection easy and light unto you. And see if it do not prove that you are more afraid than hurt. Christ will not suffer anybody to lose by him, at last. Nay you shall be a certain and a great gainer by it, both in this world, and in the world to come.

WILLIAM.   As my brother hath said, I acknowledge this to be (in appearance at least) a strong temptation. This was the temptation of Josias, that drew him to his apostasy. He forsook his praying people, and adhered unto those who did not pray to God. But this was because his own heart did not love praying to God, and did better like of the wicked ways of the non-praying Indians. But what got he at last by adhering to the worst sort of his subjects? When he was in distress they all forsook him, which his praying subjects would not have done, if he would have adhered unto them. Likewise this very thing which you propose was a temptation to Cutshamoquin. His praying to God did make such of his people as loved not that way, to waver in their subjection to him, and it did begin to make him waver in the matter of praying to God. But God did mercifully preserve him, and kept him steadfast to his dying day. But this he did, he went sometimes among them, he used them kindly, he treated them with gentle persuasion, without compulsion. By such ways he so carried the matter that they forsook him not. And I do not doubt but that the matter may be so ordered and carried, that you may be secured from that danger, which seemeth to lie in your objection. But indeed the true reason why sundry of Cutshamoquin his men left him, whereby he fell under poverty, was this. He sold unto the English all our lands which lay by the sea side and salt water save only one field. And then it was that they went to such other places as they liked better. And this one field also Josias sold away. And the inland place where we now live, Mr. Eliot procured for us, after we prayed to God.

But let the worst of your fears come to pass. Suppose all your subjects that hate praying to God should leave you. What shall you lose by it? You are rid of such as by their sins vitiate others, and multiply transgression, and provoke the wrath of God against you and yours. But consider what you shall gain by praying to God. Do not trouble yourself by poring upon what you shall lose, which at most is but a very small matter. Turn your eye to the other side, and look upon what you shall gain. You lose a few wicked men which hate praying to God. But if you pray to God, all the praying Indians will rejoice at it, and be your friends, and they are not a few, now, by the grace and blessing of Jesus Christ. All the Massachuset Indians will be your friends. All the praying Indians in the Nipmuk country will be your friends. All the praying Indians of Nope will be your friends. All the praying Indians of Nantucket will be your friends. All the praying Indians of Mahshepog, and all eastward from them as far as Cape Cod, all these will be your friends. And what comparison is betwixt these and those you lose?

Again, suppose you lose a few subjects that hate praying to God, but yet you shall gain a more intimate love of the Governor, and Magistrates, and good people of Plymouth, who were ever good friends to your father Onsamequin,[45] and to you hitherto. But if you pray to God, you shall find deference. They will more honor, respect, and love you, than ever they did. They will embrace you as a brother in Jesus Christ. Yea, farther, the Governor and Magistrates of the Massachusetts will own you, and be fatherly and friendly to you. The commissioners of the United Colonies will own you. Yea more, the King of England, and the great peers who are heads of the Corporation there, who yearly send over means to encourage and promote our praying to God, they will take notice of you. And what are a few of your subjects that hate praying to God, in comparison of all these? Yea moreover, and above all these considerations, that which is said, Luke 15:7, I tell you, there shall be joy in heaven over one poor sinner that repenteth. So that God in heaven, Jesus Christ, the Holy Ghost, and the holy angels in heaven, will joy at your turning to God. Cease therefore these vain fears of losing a few sinful people, who possibly may forsake you, if you pray unto God.

KEIT. I am drowned and overwhelmed with the weight of your reasonings. I know not what to answer you at the present. Yet I fear, that when I am out of the sunshine of your wise discourses, I shall again be plunged into the pit of doubting, by my manifold fears that do encompass me.

ANTHONY. Go on therefore and produce all your doubts. Let us see what weight is in them. Sands are heavy when many are

laid together, but bring them out one by one, and they will be
found light, and of no value. Our desire is to deal fully with
you, and hear all that you have to say. Cobwebs may seem
thick, and strong until they be handled. But when they be
touched and opened, they will be found altogether weak.

KEIT. I perceive that in your praying to God, and in your
churches, all are brought to an equality. Sachems and people
they are all fellow brethren in your churches. Poor and rich are
equally privileged. The vote of the lowest of the people hath
as much weight as the vote of the sachem. Now I doubt that
this way will lift up the heart of the poor to too much boldness,
and debase the rulers to low. This bringing all to an equality
will bring all to a confusion.

ANTHONY. This also I confess is a great and weighty point,
and must be looked upon with much prudence and caution.
The weight of a vote lieth not so much in the man, as in the
matter wherein he voteth. A poor wise man may give a better
reason than a rich man or ruler, and then it is the reason that
prevaileth, not the man. We must all be ruled by the word of
God, both sachems and people. The Word of God in the mouth
of a poor man must be regarded for the words sake, and not
for the mans sake, be he rich or poor. The management of
church liberties is a narrow edge, and may easily miscarry, and
prove hurtful; which difficulty must be helped by good conduct.
The well ordering of a church is a point of great wisdom and
care. But we must not therefore fly off from a rule, because it
is difficult. But it must be acted with the more fear, care,
and prayer.

There is such a rule in the gospel way of the churches, as
equality of vote among believers in the matters of Jesus Christ.
And herein is a great point of self-denial in sachems and chief
men, to be equal to his brethren in the things that appertain
to Christ, who is no respecter of persons. So it is said, Colos-
sians 3:11, Where there is neither Greek nor Jew, circumcision
nor uncircumcision, Barbarian, Scythian, bond nor free: but
Christ is all, and in all. And as faith makes all believers equal
in Christ, so doth the order of the gospel. All that are in gospel

order are equally concerned in the affairs of Jesus Christ. And this should not be a trouble, but a comfort and joy to every one. And therefore it is said, James 1:9, 10, Let the brother of low degree rejoice in that he is exalted; but the rich in that he is made low; for by both these Christ is exalted and in that we must rejoice.

WILLIAM.   All that my brother hath said is weighty. I will add a word further to the edge of your objection. Church order doth not abolish civil order, but establish it. Religion teacheth and commandeth reverence and obedience to civil rulers. And when a religious ruler doth deny himself for Christ his sake, to be equal with his brethren in church order, it obligeth all godly hearts the more to honor him in his civil order. I Timothy 6:2, the Lord saith, And they that have believing masters, let them not despise them, because they are brethren; but rather do them service, because they are faithful and beloved, partakers of the benefit. These things teach and exhort. Do not fear any loss of honor by submitting to gospel community in church order. But know that it is the rightest way to true honor. The hearts of all will honor those rulers that are humble and holy.

And when you shall do this for the honor of Christ, then Christ will take care to honor such rulers. For God hath promised, I Samuel 2:30, *Them that honor me, I will honor.* Believe the word of God, for you shall find it true.

KEIT.   What second thoughts may come into my mind I cannot tell. But at present I find nothing in my mind to oppose against what you say. But yet there is another thing that I am much afraid of, and that is your church admonitions and excommunications. I hear that your sachems are under that yoke. I am a sinful man as well as others, but if I must be admonished by the church, who are my subjects, I know not how I shall like that. I doubt it will be a bitter pill, too hard for me to get down and swallow.

ANTHONY.   Still your objections are great and weighty. Sin is the sickness of the soul even as diseases are the sickness of the body. Admonitions in the Lord, by the holy scriptures, are the physic of the soul, even as outward medicines are physic to the body. Now if your body be sick, you will not refuse physic because it is bitter or sharp, and difficult to bear. No, but you will bear it patiently, because you know it is wholesome, and a means to cure your sickness. The same I say about the sickness of your soul. That medicine which God hath appointed to purge away your sin, you must patiently submit unto, because it is wholesome and good for your soul. Yea, and you must be so much the more careful and willing to submit thereunto, by how much the danger of soul sicknesses are deeper and greater than bodily sicknesses be. A bodily sickness, at the worst, doth but kill the body. But soul sicknesses, if not cured, do damn both soul and body in hell, with the Devil and his angels forever. It is a desperate danger to let soul sickness go uncured. It is pleasant and delightful to the flesh to sin without control, but remember what the end of it will be. Solomon that wise king saith, Ecclesiastes 11:9, Rejoice, O young man, in thy youth; and let thy heart cheer thee in the days of thy youth, and walk in the ways of thine heart, and in the sight of thine eyes: but know thou, that for all these things God will bring thee into judgement. This is a trembling word. Felix a great ruler trembled when he heard that word, Acts 24:24. It is therefore against all wisdom to refuse to be subject to soul physic. It is a great mercy when God giveth a skilfull physician to cure our bodies. But it is a greater mercy to have a skilfull physician to heal and cure our souls. This therefore is so far from being a discouragement from praying to God, as that it is rather an encouragement. Make haste to come into that way which provideth well for your souls health, because eternal salvation dependeth upon it.

WILLIAM. I am willing to add a word or two by way of lenitive.[46] Though the matter be harsh and bitter, yet the manner of applying must be with all reverence, gentleness, meekness, tenderness, and love, so as to avoid all exasperation or provocation. So the Lord hath commanded, Galatians 6:1, Brethren, if a man be overtaken in a fault, ye which are spiritual, restore such a one in the spirit of meekness; considering thyself, lest thou also be tempted.

And for your further encouragement, we find in the scripture that great kings and rulers have meekly submitted to this soul physic. David was sharply reproved by the prophet, and he meekly submitted to it, II Samuel 12. And so it was with Eli, I Samuel 2:27. Let it not therefore be unacceptable unto you, to imitate so great, so good examples. If sachems might sin, and no body might admonish them, because they be rulers, and the ministers and people are the subjects, it were the most miserable condition in the world to be a sachem or a ruler. They would run to hell without control, and no body may say unto him, why do you so? It is said Isaiah 30:33, *For Tophet is ordained of old, yea for the king it is prepared.* If God have ordained hell for sachems, then sure he hath ordained means to keep them out of it, as well as for other men. For *God desireth not the death of a sinner, but rather that he should repent and live.* If therefore you desire to escape hell, and go to heaven, submit your soul to such means as God hath appointed to bring you to repentance and salvation. When you put the objection, you said you are a sinful man as well as others. Therefore your own heart will tell you that you have need of such helps as God hath appointed to bring you to repentance, else you cannot be saved.

KEIT.   I feel your words sink into my heart and stick there. You speak arrows. I feel that you wound me, but I do not think you hurt me. Nor do you mean me any hurt, but good. I desire to ponder and consider of these things. I have more matters to object, but I will forbear at this time. And besides, it is time for you to eat, and to take rest, and therefore I will proceed no further at this time.

ANTHONY.   We thankfully accept your patience thus long, and your good acceptance of what we say. God hath been present with us, and we perceive that the spirit of God is at work in your heart. This putteth us in hopes of a good issue.

We have one request unto you, beloved sachem, that while

we abide in your house, we may have liberty to carry ourselves like praying Indians. Namely, that when we eat, we may pray and give thanks to God, before and after meat; also before we lie down at night, and when we rise up in the morning we may pray and give thanks to God; and that discourses may be grave, and for edification; that there may be no games or sports, or such other things, which we have abandoned.

KEIT. I do like well what you say. All things shall be as you desire. It will be a good opportunity for us to see what manner of conversation you praying Indians use. I will propose it unto so many of my people as be here present, how they like of this last motion you make of allowing you free liberty of all such exercises as you praying Indians practice. What say you, my friends, to this last motion of theirs?

ALL. We like it very well, and shall willingly give attendance unto their prayers. And besides, it is not long to their sabbath. We desire they would stay the sabbath, and teach publicly, and let us see their sabbath conversation also. It may be we shall see so much beauty and desirableness in their ways that it may much heighten and raise our affections to embrace and submit our selves unto this way of praying to God.

KEIT. You go too fast. Your answer goes beyond my proposal or their request. We spake only of private conversation. I said nothing of the sabbath, nor of their public teaching. This is a greater matter. But go to, seeing you have made the motion. I will not refuse it. What say you my friends? You hear what these people desire. Will you tarry the sabbath among us and teach publicly among my people? For if you accept the motion, we shall take a course to give notice thereof to all parts of the town.

ANTHONY. We are sent by the church in the name of Jesus Christ, to call you up unto the way which leadeth to heaven. One part of this heavenly way is to keep the sabbath day, by exercising our selves in the word of God and prayer. I perceive the forwardness of your people hereunto, and your own wary condescendence unto their desires, which amounteth unto more than a calling unto us to attend the motion. It addeth encouragement and hope of good acceptance with man, and a divine blessing from heaven.

PHILIP KEITASSCOT   ANTHONY   WILLIAM   SACHEM

KEIT.   I have so ordered my occasions that they will give way to my attendance to the matter you have come about. Therefore this afternoon I have set apart, that we may have further conference about them.

The former points we discoursed, I am willing they should still lie soaking in my heart and mind. I am not ready to make replies, or to draw forth any speech about them. I choose rather to draw forth some of my other doubts and objections. Unto which, if your answers be as considerable and weighty, as they were to my former doubts, I shall then see cause to lay them up also a soaking, and pondering in my heart. Know this, that in the rowlings of my thoughts, the disquiet turnings and tumblings of my mind, do oft times molest me with variety of passions. I am sometimes in grief and anguish of mind, especially when I over look my life past, and remember the many sins and follies that I have stained my life and honor withall. I think with myself, what a fool have I been, that for the love of a lust, which dogs and brute creatures delight in, that I, a man, a sachem, should be so besotted, as to stain my honor, wound my soul, offend God, and expose my self to eternal damnation. And all this for a short delight that is gone with a blast, and leaves nothing behind but shame and sorrow; and these are durable and indelible, a sad effect of sensual pleasure. Ah what a fool have I been when I should have employed myself in higher and greater matters for the honor of God, and the good of my people. I have wasted my precious time and strength to satiate my pleasures, which have left such a sting and torment in my soul, which all my estate and honor cannot ease me of. But they are like to torment me forever. I am never without wicked company to draw me out unto such iniquities. But none of them can ease the torment of my mind and conscience, though some apply themselves so to do. I do find their remedies are false and uneffectual.

But I have quite lost my self. I did not intend to open and pour out my mind and thoughts about these matters; but full vessels are ready to run over. I will come to that which I did intend.

ANTHONY.   Beloved sachem, as the overflowings of your grief have interrupted your intended discourse, so let me take so much boldness to lengthen this your interruption, with a word of God that may, by his blessing, be (at least) the beginning of a cordial to your heart, and a cure to your stain and wound. Sin is a shame to any nation or person, but repentance is an honor. Your griefs have the right favor of repentance. It is said, I Corinthians 3:18 *Let a man become a fool, that he may be wise.* You chide yourself for your folly. You do well so to do. It is an act of wisdom so to do. Go on in this frame of heart, and be constant, and you shall find rest. Christ calleth troubled souls to come unto him, Matthew 11:28, and he promiseth to give them rest, and he is able to perform his promise. In his hand I leave this matter, and your tossed soul with inward griefs, that in him you may find rest.

WILLIAM.   My brother hath presented you with a cordial for your heart grief. I will present you with some balm to heal your soul wounds. It is said, Jeremiah 8:22, Is there no balm in Gilead? Is there no physician there? Why then is not the health of the daughter of my people recovered? Behold, in God's word we find a balm for wounded souls, and that is the death and blood of Jesus Christ, believed by faith. For Christ hath died for our sins, and rose again from the dead for our justification. He offereth a pardon for all your sins, and he will heal your soul, and quiet your heart from all those turmoiling troubles and griefs. Believe therefore in Jesus Christ, and he will pardon and save you.

KEIT. I thank you for these comfortable words. I feel them in my heart, and I desire to lay them up among other things which I ponder in my heart.

And now I will proceed to open such other doubts which lie in my mind as impediments which hinder me, and delay me from accepting of this way of praying to God. I perceive in all your discourses, that you have a book which you call *The Word of God,* and you read it to me. I perceive also that in your worshipping of God morning and night, you read in that book. I pray tell me what book that is? What is written in it? And how do you know that it is the Word of God? Many say that some wise Englishmen have devised and framed it, and tell us that it is God's word, when as it is no other than the words of wise men.

Hoh! We shall be interrupted in our discourse. For here cometh in a sachem that hateth praying to God, and hath been a means of delaying my entrance into this way. But if he come up unto us, we will go on and let him be partaker of our discourse, if he like of it, and be willing so to do.

Ehoh, my friend. I pray come and sit down here, and harken to our discourse. Here be some of the Massachuset praying Indians, who are soliciting me to pray unto God. And we are now discoursing about a book which they have, which they say is the Word of God. And I am now enquiring of them what is contained in that book, and how it may be made appear that it is the Word of God? If you think good to join with us in this discourse, it will be acceptable unto us to have your company, and to hear what you have to say about it.

SACHEM. I am willing to be present and hear your discourse. But as for this new way of praying to God, I like it not. We and our forefathers have through all generations lived in our religion, which I desire not to change. Are we wiser than our forefathers? And I like not to suffer our people to read that book which they call the Word of God. If it be God's word, it is too deep for ignorant people to meddle withall. And it will fill them with new light and notions, which withdraws them from our obedience, and leadeth them to make trouble and disturbance unto us, in those old ways in which we and our forefathers have walked. And my counsel is to suppress the reading of that book.

ANTHONY. With due respect unto you, Sachem, I shall thus answer unto what you say. If a great sachem in a far country should send unto you a writing, wherein he giveth you wise counsel, would you not read it? Would you not hear what he saith? And would you not suffer your people to learn wisdom, but continue in their ignorance and blindness? Sure you would show so much respect to a man, a sachem, that so do so kindly to you. Now so it is, that the great God who made these high heavens, and the great lights that be therein; who made this earth, and all this great world, and all things in it; who is king of kings, and Lord of lords: I say this great God, pitying to see the ignorance that all men are darkened withall, he hath sent us his word, which will make wise the ignorant. And will you not suffer your people to learn that wisdom? Do you love darkness better than light?

Besides, all mankind live in the ways of sin, which lead them to hell torments, where they shall be punished with eternal fire. But God pitying this miserable condition of man, hath sent us this word of his, which showeth us the way to escape hell torments, and leadeth us into the way that leadeth us to eternal life, happiness, and glory. And will not you suffer your people to learn this good way, when God offereth it unto us? Consider how your people will curse you, when they feel these torments, because you would not suffer them to learn the true way to heaven and happiness. And what though we are not wiser than our forefathers, yet God can teach us such wisdom as our forefathers did not know. I think, that we are bound to think that our fathers were so wise, that if God's word had been brought and offered to them, they would have received it, and would have learned by it to be wiser than they were. And why therefore should not we be so wise, as to do that which our wise fathers would have done, if this light had shined unto them, as it now doth unto us. Let not the deepness of that wisdom in God's word hinder us that are ignorant from searching into it, for by reading of God's word the ignorant may be made wise, Psalm 19:7, The law of God is perfect, converting the soul: the testimony of the Lord is sure, making wise the simple. David learned to be wise by reading the Word of God, wiser than his enemies, wiser than his teachers, wiser than the ancients, Psalm 119: 98-100, and so may we. It is a vain word to say, they are ignorant, and therefore they may not read the word. The contrary to this is true. Because they are ignorant, therefore let them search and read the Word of God, because it will make them wise. But you give the reason that lieth in the bottom of your heart, when you say, by reading of the word they will learn new light, which will molest and trouble them that love and walk in their old lusts, and deeds of darkness. And therefore you will keep them from the light. But I pray consider at what a dear rate you purchase your quiet in your old ways of sin and darkness, which lead you to hell, when you will compel all your people to live in sin and darkness, for fear lest when they find the light of God's word, they should molest and trouble you in your lusts and sins.

WILLIAM.   I will add a few words to what my brother hath spoken. I have heard that in the other part of the world there be a certain people who are called Papists, whose ministers and teachers live in all manner of wickedness and lewdness, and permit and teach the people so to do. And these wicked ministers will not suffer the people to read the Word of God, and pretend the same reason as you do, because they be ignorant. But the true reason is the same which you plainly speak out, lest by the knowledge of the word, they should have light to see into their vileness, and molest them in their lusts and sins. And they are so cruel, that if they find anyone that readeth the Word of God, they will kill him. They choose rather to lead all their people with them to hell, than to suffer them to see the light whereby they may be saved. Lest when they see the light, they should discover their filthiness, and trouble them in their way to hell. But God doth account these men murderers, and hath threatened to bring upon them fearful destruction, to revenge the blood of God's people whom they have murdered. Therefore I pray you to consider, that the like vengeance from God will fall upon you, if you will not suffer your people to search into, and learn the word of God.

KEIT.   What you have said hath fully settled and satisfied my heart in this point. I will never hinder my people from the knowledge of the Word of God, and I wonder at those vile ministers that do so wickedly abuse the people. And I wonder at the sachems, that they will suffer such vile ministers to abuse their people in that manner, why do they not suppress them? And why do they not command their people to print the Bible, and let it be free for any man that will buy them, and read them? I wonder at these things. Can you satisfy me in the reason thereof?

WILLIAM.   I can say but little to it. Only thus much have I heard. Some sachems are as bad as the ministers, and of the same mind with their ministers. They are like minded as this sachem is. Other sachems that are wiser and better minded, yet they cannot help it, because their ministers are so rich, and by that means have so many people depending on them, that their sachems dare not meddle with them. And their ministers take a cunning course to keep themselves and their successors rich, for they will not suffer one another to marry, whereby they should have lawful children to inherit their riches. But when they die, the next minister hath all, or most of the riches that he had. And to the end they may keep one another from marrying, they suffer one another to keep whores, so that they have bastards good store, but no lawful children. And by this means they maintain themselves in very great wealth, so that the sachems dare not meddle with them.

KEIT.   Doth nobody see these base doings of these ministers?

WILLIAM.   Oh yes, many. But if anybody speak a word against them, they will kill him presently, so that partly by their wealth, and partly by their cruelty, they keep everybody in fear of them.

KEIT.   Oh strange! How many of these wicked ministers be there, that they are so potent?

WILLIAM.   Oh, a great many. The ministers of I know not how many countries combine together, and be of one mind, to uphold one another; and they choose one chief, and call him a Pope, and say that he has power to pardon men's sins and will sell pardons, for money, and by that means they get a great deal of wealth. For people are such fools as to think that he can pardon them, when as the Popes be as vile sinners as anybody, and keep whores, and get bastards. Other of these ministers they call Cardinals; others Lord Archbishop; others Lord Bishop; other, Lord Abbot; others, Lord Friar, and I cannot tell how many more. And many of these as rich as sachems, and leave their wealth to their successors, because they have no lawful children, only keep whores, and get bastards. And they will allow their sachems or anybody else, to keep whores, and get bastards, and the Pope will pardon them for money. And this that I tell you, is but a little of the filthiness that is among these wicked ministers. Now if people should but look into the Word of God, they would presently find, that God has appointed no such ministers as these. They are all of them the Devil's ministers, and not God's. And if sachems and people knew this, they would buy no more pardons of them, and the sachems would suppress them, and take away their great riches, or employ them to better uses. And for this reason they will not suffer any but themselves to read the scripture. They will kill them if they do. And they have Lords Inquisitors, as they call them, to watch and search if anybody have a Bible, or any other good book, that opens and discovers their villainy, he shall be killed. And these Lords Inquisitors are as rich as sachems. And thus they keep all men in subjection to them, and in fear of them, and sachems are afraid of them, and they do what they list.

KEIT. Here be ministers with all my heart! Are these the men that manage their religion? These are worse than our pauwaus. If any pauwau in my dominions should be half this vile, I would scourge him. I see that in some places of the world there be worse men than we Indians be. I do not think there is such vileness to be found among any of the Indians in all this country. What may be further off I know not. And if all this vileness be maintained by ignorance of the Word of God, it seemeth to me, that it is a principal thing in religion to know and be acquainted with the Word of God. And therefore I desire that now we may go on with our intended discourse. And whereas I proposed two questions, me thinks that much may be gathered out of this discourse we have had, tending to show what matter is contained in the Word of God. But it is like you will speak more fully to it. I shall therefore bend my mind to give attendance unto what you shall further say.

ANTHONY. This question is one great principle in religion. And I cannot take a surer and better course to answer it, then by declaring the answer that is given in our catechism unto the question, and by opening some of the texts of scripture which are there brought for the proof and manifestation thereof.

The question is: What is the Word of God? The answer is: It is the will of God written in the Bible, whereby he rightly guideth man, in everything in this world, and whereby he bringeth us to eternal salvation. These are but few words, but full of weight, and proved by divers scriptures.

KEIT. What do you mean by scripture?

ANTHONY. The word and will of God written in a book, whereby we not only hear it with our ears, when it is spoken by others, but we may see it with our eyes, and read the writing ourselves. And this is a great benefit to us, to have God's word and will written. For a word spoken is soon gone, and nothing retaineth it but our memory, and that impression which it made upon our mind and heart. But when this word is written in a book, there it will abide, though we have forgotten it. And we may

read it over a thousand times, and help our weak memories,
so that it shall never be forgotten. Yea, and such as cannot have
an opportunity of hearing the word, yet they may always have
an opportunity of reading the word, because it is written in the
Bible; which they have by them in their houses, and may read
in it night and day. We do therefore call the Word of God scripture, because it is written in a book.

KEIT.   I am satisfied in what you say. I pray go on to open
those texts of scripture which the catechism giveth for proofs.

ANTHONY.   The first text I mention is Hosea 8:12. *I have
written to him the great things of my law, but they were counted
as a strange thing.* Here God gives to man a law, and he writeth
this law, and every thing in this law is *a great matter.* Though
some things are greater than others, yet every thing that God
hath written is a great matter. But God doth blame men for
counting them as *strange things.* We should be well acquainted
with them.
     Daniel 10:21. When an angel spake to Daniel, he told him,
that *he would declare to him that which is noted in the scriptures of truth.* And we that teach others most carefully so do,
we must teach nothing but that which is noted in, and grounded
upon the scriptures of truth. And we need to teach nothing else,
for all things needful for salvation are contained in the scriptures, as appears II Timothy 3:16, 17. All scripture is given by
inspiration of God, and is profitable for doctrine, for reproof,
for correction, for instruction in righteousness: that the man
of God may be perfect, thoroughly furnished unto all good
works. The man of God here, meaneth, or may be applied to
walk by the rule of the word, be he a sachem, or a teacher, or
a father, etc. Every man may find in the scriptures a perfect
rule to guide him in every thought, word or deed. So that the
Word of God is a perfect law to guide every man, in every
thing, all the days of his life. And the Word of God is not only
a rule to guide us in this life but it also brings us to heaven;
Acts 20:32. And now, brethren, I commend you to God, and
to the word of his grace, which is able to build you up, and to

give you an inheritance among all them which are sanctified. And James 1:21, Wherefore lay apart all filthiness and superfluity of naughtiness, and receive with meekness the engrafted word, which is able to save your souls. Many such testimonies I might add, to show the fulness of the perfection of the word of God. But I forbear at present.

WILLIAM.   I will add a few words touching the perfection of the scriptures. Deuteronomy 12:32, What thing soever I command you, observe to do it: thou shalt not add thereto, nor diminish from it. Here be two ways of wronging the scriptures: 1. By adding to it; 2. By taking from it. Now these popish teachers and ministers of whom I did discourse before, they do most wickedly wrong the scriptures, especially by adding to them. They say that their offices are commanded in the scripture, and that the Pope is Christ his vicar, and that he hath power to pardon sin, and abundance more such rotten stuff they add unto the scripture.

Now this is another reason why they will not suffer people to read the scriptures, because then everybody would find out their false dealing. And therefore if anybody find them out, they will presently kill them. The great wrong they do unto the scriptures of truth is one of their great sins. They add their own wicked inventions unto the pure and perfect Word of God.

KEIT.   Your discourse doth breed in my heart an admiration at that excellent book. And I find in my heart a longing desire to be acquainted with that book, and with those excellent matters that are contained in it. But although my heart doth begin to reverence that book for the sake of the matter contained in it, yet I desire that you would proceed to give me your ground, why you did believe that it is God's word, because I shall then reverence the word, not only for the matters sake, but also the authors sake. Good words spoken by a good man do obtain respect; much more may the words that God speaketh command all reverence.

ANTHONY.   This point also being a great principle in religion,

I will take the same course in it as I did in the former. I will
show you what answer we are taught in our catechism, and I
will touch some of the proofs.

1. The first reason to prove the scriptures to be the
Word of God is because they teach us the first creation of the
world, and all things in it, which no man nor angel doth know
or can teach, only God. And this is proved in the first chapter
of Genesis, where we read the wonderful work of God in the
creation of the world, when man was last made.

2. The second reason is from the holiness and perfection of the Word of God. No man or angel could give so holy,
pure, and perfect a law, as God's law is, Psalm 19:8-11. Also
Psalm 12:6, *The words of the Lord are pure words: as silver
tried in a furnace of earth, purified seven times.*

3. The third reason is, because the word of the Lord is
confirmed by such miracles, as only God himself is able to perform. Moses the first writer of scripture, did many great miracles in Egypt, in the Red Sea, and in the wilderness. So did
many other prophets. But especially Jesus Christ did many
wonderful miracles, and so did the Apostles, by which our
faith is confirmed, that their writings are the Word of God.

4. Because the scriptures doth reveal unto us Jesus
Christ, and salvation by Christ, according to the gospel of Jesus
Christ. This no man or angel could ever have found out, only
God. II Corinthians 5:19, To wit, that God was in Christ, reconciling the world unto himself, not imputing their trespasses
unto them; and hath committed unto us the word of reconciliation. John 5:39, Search the scriptures; for in them ye think
ye have eternal life: and they are they which testify of me.
Therefore they are the Word of God.

5. Because the Word of God doth convert the soul from
sin and Satan, unto God. It sanctifies the soul, and doth lead
men's souls in the ways of life, unto salvation. It is the sword
of the spirit to conquer the Devil. James 1:18, Of his own will
begat he us with the word of truth, that we should be a kind
of firstfruits of his creatures. John 17:17, Sanctify them through
thy truth: thy word is truth. Ephesians 6:17, And take the hel-

met of salvation, and the sword of the Spirit, which is the Word of God. Such grounds as these we are taught in our catechism.[47]

KEIT. Who can oppose or gainsay the mountainous weight of these arguments? I am more than satisfied. I am ashamed of my ignorance, and I abhor myself that ever I doubted of this point. And I desire wholly to give myself to the knowledge of, and obedience to the Word of God, and to abandon and forsake these sins which the Word of God reproveth and condemneth.

WILLIAM. I will add one consideration further, to maintain that the scriptures are the Word of God; and that is, by the great antiquity of these writings; which have been extant so many thousands of years, and have sailed through so many enemies hands, who have used all art and force to abolish them, or corrupt them, and yet they could never do it. Moses wrote the first five books of scripture above a thousand and four hundred years before Christ came, and it is above a thousand and six hundred years since Christ came, and since the gospel, the last part of the scripture, was written. Put these two numbers together and they make three thousand years. So long the church have had the scriptures. And all this while the Devil and wicked men have endeavored either to abolish them, or corrupt them, but they could never do it. We have every word of God perfect and pure unto this day, which cannot be said of any other writing in all the world. And this wonderful divine protection of this book doth greatly manifest that doubtless it is God's own word, over which he hath bestowed such eminent care.

KEIT. But how do you know all this? How do you know what was done so many thousand years ago?

WILLIAM. The scriptures themselves have kept a perfect record of times from the beginning of the world unto the coming of Christ, and out of that chronology we may perfectly know how long Moses was before Christ. And there be other sure ways to

know how many years it is since Christ came. And thus may
we know certainly how long the scriptures have been written.

KEIT. If this be so, the reason is strong. The antiquity of the
book requireth reverence, and God's constant care of it showeth
he hath a divine influence in it.

But we are now called off from any further proceedings in
our discourse at this time. Before we part, I have one motion
and request to propose unto you. Tomorrow is your sabbath,
and I have a desire that you two would teach us that day and
let us see the manner how you worship God. It may please God
to make more of his light to shine among us. You remember
what passed about this motion. I do now with more desire con-
firm that motion.

ANTHONY. We also are still of the same mind and purpose,
and are the more confirmed in our hearts, because we see that
God is on the coming hand, to incline your heart unto the Lord.

AFTER THE SABBATH
PHILIP KEITASSCOT   ANTHONY   WILLIAM

KEIT. I have now lived one sabbath. Many a sabbath have I
been dead, and followed works of darkness and sin, when I
should have been following the Lord in such ways of worship,
as yesterday was spent in. I am wounded at my heart to remember what I have done upon the sabbath day. I have served
the Devil, and lust and sins of all sorts, even upon the sabbath
days. The sins that I have committed do render me vile in the
sight of God, and the time wherein I have committed many of
them, doth render me more vile in the eyes of the Lord my
judge. You said yesterday, that Christ Jesus is the Lord of the
sabbath, and requires all men to spend that day in his service.
And when Christ Jesus shall judge the world, he will examine
all men how they spent every sabbath. Oh wretched man that

I am. What answer shall I make? Though I am a sachem here
on earth, I shall be but a subject in the day of judgment. I
now sit upon the bench to judge others, then I must stand at
the bar to be judged myself. Oh what mountains of sin have I
heaped up in my wicked life! I had forgot my sins, and I thought
God had forgot them too. And I had thought my conscience
had forgot them also, but now I see it is not so. God hath numbered all my ways, my thoughts, my words and works, and I
feel now that my conscience remembereth them also; though
it hath been asleep in the times of my ignorance and profane-
ness, yea of all sin; and in particular of this great sin of profaning the sabbath. My heart is wounded with the sense of this sin
especially, and that forceth my troubled conscience to gall and
afflict my soul with the remembrance of all my sins. But why
say I all? I now find my sins are numberless. My own personal
sins are many, great and vile. My heart doth loathe my self to
remember them. They make me an abhoring to God. But moreover and besides, my own personal sins, other men's sins I am
guilty of. Oh how many have sinned upon my account, many
ways? I am a sachem over my people, to rule them in virtue,
and to do them good. But I have done contrary to my charge.
I have led them out into all sin, and thereby I have done them
the greatest hurt and mischief. I have been a means of their
damnation. Oh how many are gone, and going to hell on my
account? How shall I escape damnation, who have led so many
into that eternal pit? Oh I am pained at my heart, what shall
I do? Oh what shall I do?

ANTHONY.   No creature can help you; none but God in Jesus
Christ, he can help you. Consider that text, Micah 6:6-8, Wherewith shall I come before the Lord, and bow myself before the
high God? Shall I come before him with burnt offerings, with
calves of a year old? Will the Lord be pleased with thousands
of rams, or with ten thousands of rivers of oil? Shall I give my
firstborn for my transgression, the fruit of my body for the
sin of my soul? He hath showed thee, O man, what is good:
and what doth the Lord require of thee, but to do justly, and
to love mercy, and to walk humbly with thy God? Nothing

that you can do or bring to God can pacify that divine wrath
that is kindled against you. But, verse eight, he showeth you
the way. Also consider that text, John 4:6, Now Jacob's well
was there. Jesus therefore, being wearied with his journey, sat
thus on the well: and it was about the sixth hour. You have
been a great sinner. Now you lament it. You would obtain a
pardon, and be reconciled to God. This word of God showeth
you the way, and that is to humble yourself before Christ
Jesus, believe in him, and give up yourself to be his servant,
yourself to worship the Lord, and to bring on all your people
to do the same. I remember two places in Daniel where sachems
were in trouble of mind, as you now are, and Daniel gave
them counsel from the Lord. The first place is Daniel 4:27,
Wherefore, O king, let my counsel be acceptable unto thee,
and break off thy sins by righteousness, and thine iniquities
by showing mercy to the poor; if it may be a lengthening of
thy tranquillity. And my heart is persuaded (with submission
to the Lord) that if you now turn unto God, and promote praying to God among all your people, you shall see better days
than ever you have yet seen. There is another sad story in the
fifth chapter of Daniel, where the wicked sachem did act pro-
fanely against the God of heaven, and then appeared fingers
which wrote *Mene, Mene, Tekel Upharsin.* But let the interpretation of that be unto your enemies, and not to you, beloved
sachem. I say unto you in that word of the Lord, Acts 16:31,
And they said, Believe on the Lord Jesus Christ, and thou shalt
be saved, and thy house.

WILLIAM.   Hope of relief is a means to ease grief and to raise
the distressed heart to apply itself unto means of remedy. In
the second of Chronicles 33, we read of a sachem that was a
greater sinner than you have been. Yet upon his repentance
and change of life, he obtained mercy. His name was Manasseh.
His sins were such as that it is an abhoring to read them. Then
God brought him into affliction, and it is said, verse 12, 13,
And when he was in affliction, he besought the Lord his God,
and humbled himself greatly before the God of his fathers.
And prayed unto him: and he was entreated of him, and heard
his supplication, and brought him again to Jerusalem into his

kingdom. Then Manasseh knew that the Lord he was God. So
I say unto you, beloved sachem, humble yourself before the
Lord. Set up praying to God among all your people, walk in
ways of wisdom and religion, and you shall find that God will
be merciful to you, and your latter days shall be blessed, and
be a blessing.

KEIT.   Words that come swimming in love, with full sails of
wisdom, have great power to calm heart storms of grief and
trouble. I now find it true. My soul is wounded for my sin in
profaning the sabbath day. Now I desire to look deeper into
the matter. I desire you would open unto me the sabbath, that
I may know my former sins, and further duty.

ANTHONY.   The doctrine of the sabbath is a great point in
religion. It is one of the ten moral, universal commandments
of God, which are required of all mankind; and the fourth command, a chief hinge of all the rest. By a religious keeping of
the sabbath, we act our obedience to all the commands. By
profaning the sabbath, we turn all religion and good order out
of doors, and set open a door unto all sin and wickedness, so
weighty a matter is the good keeping of the sabbath day. For
the opening of the sabbath, I know not a better way, than to
open (briefly) the fourth command; which I shall do, by laying
it out into six parts.
    1. Here is the preface, in this word, *remember the sab-
bath day*, to show the great weight and worth of the sabbath,
and our proneness to slight it; and to stablish a perpetual and
careful preparation to the sabbath. Nehemiah 13:19, And it
came to pass, that when the gates of Jerusalem began to be
dark before the sabbath, I commanded that the gates should
be shut, and charged that they should not be opened till after
the sabbath: and some of my servants set I at the gates, that
there should no burden be brought in on the sabbath day.
    2. Here is the affirmative part of the command, where-
in we are commanded to keep the whole sabbath holy, both in
thought, word, and deed. Isaiah 58:13, If thou turn away thy
foot from the sabbath, from doing thy pleasure on my holy
day; and call the sabbath a delight, the holy of the Lord, honor-

able; and shalt honor him, not doing thine own ways, nor finding thine own pleasure, nor speaking thine own words.

3. Here is an exact distribution of all time betwixt God
and man, wherein God hath appointed six parts or days to man,
and the seventh part is dedicated to God. And hence it followeth
that the sabbath was capable of being changed, from the last
of seven, to the first of seven; and so the Lord hath changed it,
I Corinthians 16:2, Acts 20:7, Revelation 1:10. And when this
change was first made, the church kept two sabbaths together,
as the Passover and the Lord's Supper were together.

4. Here is the negative part of this command, wherein
we are forbidden all our works, in word or deed: Thou shalt
do no manner of work.

5. Here be the persons that be bound to keep the sabbath, *all*, high and low, rich and poor, male and female, in all
societies and relations, and strangers, thou, thy son, thy daughter,
thy man servant, thy maid servant, thy cattle, and thy stranger.

6. Here be three reasons to urge us to a reverent and
careful keeping of the sabbath.

1. Taken from God's most holy and wise example,
who six days created, but on the seventh day rested in his heavenly joys.

2. The second reason is, because God hath put a
blessing on the head of the sabbath, and on all that keep it holy.
He blessed the seventh day.

3. The third reason is, because the Lord made it
holy. He dedicated it to holy use, and therefore may not be
violated without sacrilege. Malachi 3:8, Will ye rob God? Thus
have I opened this command.

WILLIAM. I will only add two texts of scripture; Jeremiah
17:19 to end, Thus said the Lord unto me; Go and stand in the
gate of the children of the people, whereby the kings of Judah
come in, and by the which they go out, and in all the gates of
Jerusalem. The other text is Exodus 31:13-17, Speak thou also
unto the children of Israel, saying, Verily my sabbaths ye shall
keep: for it is a sign between me and you throughout your
generations; that ye may know that I am the Lord that doth

sanctify you. Ye shall keep the sabbath therefore; for it is holy
unto you: every one that defileth it shall surely be put to death:
for whosoever doeth any work therein, that soul shall be cut
off from among his people. Six days may work be done; but in
the seventh is the sabbath of rest, holy to the Lord; whosoever
doeth any work in the sabbath day, he shall surely be put to
death. Wherefore the children of Israel shall keep the sabbath,
to observe the sabbath throughout their generations, for a perpetual convenant. It is a sign between me and the children of
Israel for ever: for in six days the Lord made heaven and earth,
and on the seventh day he rested, and was refreshed.

KEIT.   I am now in a great strait. My heart is bent within me
to keep the sabbaths. But alas, neither I nor any of my people
know how to do it, unless we have somebody to teach us.

ANTHONY.   It is true that you say, and I return you this answer.
When we return, and make report of the grace of God poured
out upon you, and of your acceptance of the word of God,
and resolution to keep the sabbath, and your desire of a teacher,
we know that the church will presently take care to send a
teacher unto you. Or further we propose, if you and your people shall choose any one whom your soul's desire, and send
your request to the church, that he might be sent unto you, we
doubt not but the church will readily grant your desire.

PENITENT JOHN

A penitent soul in great distress cometh unto John Speen,[48]
one of the teachers of the church at Natick; where we shall
find the penitent pouring out his griefs, and John ministering
counsel and comfort.

PENIT.   Oh my friend, I am glad I have met you in so opportune
a time and place. My heart is broken with grief. I am ready to

sink into the ground because of my distressed mind. I desire
to pour out my melted heart into your loving bosom. It may
be you may give me counsel what I shall do in my distress,
and advise me if there be any way or means to comfort this
distressed soul of mine.

JOHN.   Alas, your sorrowful countenance doth indeed discover
that your mind is oppressed with grief, and in such cases men
are miserable comforters. God only knoweth how to speak a
word of comfort to the heart. He made the heart of man, he
knoweth all the sorrows and griefs thereof. And usually God
doth afflict the heart with grief, out of great love, that he
might call the distressed soul to come to him, and make its
griefs known to him. And he is very gracious and pitiful to
such afflicted souls. For Christ hath said, Matthew 11:28, Come
unto me, all ye that labor and are heavy laden, and I will give
you rest. My first counsel therefore is, that you would pray unto
God, and believe in Jesus Christ, and he will surely give you rest.
But as for man, especially such a poor creature as I am, I cannot
help you, nor is there any help for you in the hand of man.

PENIT.   But the words of a true-hearted loving friend may
minister some comfort, and I do already feel that your words
have relief in them, in that you tell me Jesus Christ is so tender-
hearted towards those that are of an afflicted spirit.

JOHN.   True it is that God hath said, *The priest's lips shall preserve knowledge, and thou shalt enquire the law at his mouth.*[49]
I am very weak, but I am willing to help your afflicted soul to
go to Jesus Christ, who will not fail to comfort you. Seeing
therefore it is your desire, let me hear your griefs and troubles.
It may please God to put a word into my mouth, whereby the
good spirit of God may speak comfort to your sorrowful heart.

PENIT.   My outward condition is full of affliction, and those
frowns from the brow of providence do make me fear that the
wrath of God is set against me and will wear away my life with

grief, and then cast me away into hell among the damned, where I shall perish forever.

JOHN. This is a wholesome fear, and you shall find it will end well. My counsel is, mingle hope with your fear, viz. that God doth outwardly afflict you, that he might drive your distressed soul into the bosom of Jesus Christ, who will graciously pardon all your sins, and save your soul from those eternal flames, which you so much dread. It is God's usual way of grace, to put his lambs into distress, that he might cause them to fly for refuge into his bosom. And I hope that it is his meaning so to deal with you, because I see that his afflicting hand doth so kindly melt your heart, and causeth you to seek refuge to save you from these everlasting burnings. These distresses will make the salvation of Christ precious unto you. Consider that text, Ecclesiastes 7:3-4, Sorrow is better than laughter: for by the sadness of the countenance the heart is made better. The heart of the wise is in the house of mourning; but the heart of fools is in the house of mirth. But what are those outward distresses which do afflict you?

PENIT. I know not where to begin or end. The world hath always promised me fair, but it hath ever failed me. My mornings have had some brightness, but my rising day is always clouded, and full of darkness. And I know not but my sun will set in thick darkness and despair. You know my father was a sachem of the blood, and I was brought up under high capacities and expectations. I have been chosen and advanced, as you know, to the degree of sachem, but so filled with crosses and distresses, that I never enjoy myself, nor one quiet day. My griefs are multiplied like the waves of the sea. They break in upon me, and are ready to overwhelm me.

JOHN. You say the world hath ever failed you, and so it always dealeth with God's children. But I will show you who will never fail you. Psalm 73:26, My flesh and my heart faileth: but God is the strength of my heart, and my portion for ever.

Let your soul ponder and feed upon this promise. See also Hebrews 13:5, Let your conversation be without covetousness; and be content with such things as ye have: for he hath said, I will never leave thee, nor forsake thee. Mark that word, never leave thee nor forsake thee; the word will hold both in this life, and to eternity.

You further say, that your bright mornings prove black and cloudy days. It hath been so with other of God's children. Read the 88th Psalm, and you shall find the prophet just in your case in many verses of that psalm. I will mention some of the words, verses 6-9. Thou hast laid me in the lowest pit, in darkness, in the deeps. Thy wrath lieth hard upon me, and thou hast afflicted me with all thy waves. Thou hast put away mine acquaintance from me; thou hast made me an abomination unto them: I am shut up, and I cannot come forth. Mine eye mourneth by reason of affliction: Lord, I have called daily upon thee, I have stretched out my hands unto thee. Behold a dear child of God in as bitter distress as you are. Yet the first sentence of this psalm is a word of faith. He saith, O Lord of my salvation. It is some comfort to a distressed soul, to have good company with them. You have the best company in the world, for you have the company of Jesus Christ. See Isaiah 53:3, He is despised and rejected of men; a man of sorrows, and acquainted with grief: and we hid as it were our faces from him; he was despised, and we esteemed him not. When you are alone by yourself, read all this chapter. You shall find that Christ was in greater distresses than you are, which he suffered patiently, to procure for us pardon and salvation, and by his suffering he had experience of sufferings, that he might pity us in our griefs. And therefore it is said, Hebrews 4:15, For we have not an high priest which cannot be touched with the feeling of our infirmities; but was in all points tempted like as we are, yet without sin. Our afflictions, alas, expose us often times to sin, but in that case also Christ is very pitiful and gracious, he remembereth that we are but dust, Psalm 103:14.

You add. You fear that your sun will set in darkness and despair. I answer to you, consider what future things belong to God. Do not afflict yourself with future things. Sufficient for the day is the evil thereof, Matthew 6:34. Let tomorrow care for itself. But suppose you should have no comfort till you die. It is the case of many of God's children to die in a dark cloud. And Christ himself satisfied this case, Matthew 27:46, 50. And about the ninth hour Jesus cried with a loud voice, saying, Eli, Eli, lama sabachthani? that is to say, My God, my God, why hast thou forsaken me? Verse 50, Jesus, when he had cried again with a loud voice, yielded up the ghost. What if some of God's children should in this point be conformed to Jesus Christ? Do not add to your sorrows, fears of a sad condition which Christ hath sanctified.

Touching your parentage, and present state, I know how it is very well. In this case I advise you to consider, that if your worldly cup had been filled with such sweetness as flesh and blood desire, it might have been much worse for your soul. A soul drowned in earthly pleasure is rarely saved. But a soul drowned in worldly sorrows and griefs, (if influenced in the knowledge of Jesus Christ) shall never be lost, because the sorrows and crosses of the world will keep him from surfeiting upon the creature, and drive him to satiate himself in Christ by the promises of the gospel. Thus have I answered to the chief points in your complaint.

PENIT.   Oh the power of the Word of God, aptly applied unto the case of a distressed soul! The sweet experience that I have now found in those scriptures which you have produced, and applied to my case, shall make me, hereafter, to search and read the scriptures more than I have done. I do, like Hagar, complain for water, when it is just by me, if I search. I hope I shall read the scriptures more than ever I have done.

JOHN.   You have prevented me, or rather the spirit of God hath put into your heart by power and grace, that which I intended to have presented to you by way of advice and counsel. Namely, to be frequent and abundant in reading the scriptures. For you see that all soul cordials are laid up there. Fetch them out therefore from that divine treasury and make use of them for your comfort. I know the Devil will oppose you in this matter, and keep you from conversing in the scriptures, because they are *the sweet sword of the spirit*, Ephesians 6:17, whereby we resist his temptations, as Christ himself hath set us an example, Matthew 4:4, 7, 10. When the Devil assaulted him with a temptation, he drew forth the sword of the spirit, a text of scripture, and opposed the temptation thereby, and that presently conquered the tempter. Do you the same. You cannot imitate a better pattern than our Lord Jesus Christ. And it is his command also that we should so do, John 5:39, *Search the scriptures.* And David made them his meditation day and night, Psalm 1:2. And he had the like experience that you now have found, and came to the like resolution, Psalm 119:93, I will never forget thy precepts, for with them thou hast quickened me.

PENIT. I feel much tranquility in my mind in this way of seeking soul comfort in the scriptures. Oh I have found out a way of refuge, comfort and rest in a stormy time. I hope the Lord will give me grace and wisdom to make more use thereof than ever I have done in my life.

But still my soul is in great doubts and fears about my eternal condition. If I spend this life in griefs and sorrows, and when I finish here, I go away to eternal misery, oh what a lamentable case is that! And my fear is that this will be my condition. My griefs indeed are many, but they are worldly sorrow. I cannot say that I am converted. I desire to know what it is to be converted.

JOHN. All mankind are once born. By natural birth they come into this world. But all God's children are born again. John 3:3, Jesus answered and said unto him, Verily, verily, I say unto thee, except a man be born again, he cannot see the kingdom of God. And this is a spiritual birth, verse 5, Jesus answered, verily, verily, I say unto thee, except a man be born of water and of the spirit, he cannot enter into the kingdom of God. Baptism is an outward sign of it, but the inward grace is the work of the spirit, and the spirit worketh by the Word of God, James 1:18, 21, Of his own will begat he us with the word of truth, that we should be a kind of firstfruits of his creatures, and verse 21,

Wherefore lay apart all filthiness and superfluity of naughtiness, and receive with meekness the engrafted word, which is able to save your souls. By faith in the promise the soul is united to Christ, and he that is joined to the Lord is one spirit, I Corinthians 6:17. When an afflicted soul doth venture itself, and its all, upon the fruitful word of promise, and says to God, as Job said, Job 13:15, Though he kill me, yet I will trust in him, this is the new born soul, and this believing soul shall be surely saved at last, whatever sorrows and afflictions it goes through in this life.

And whereas you say that your sorrows and griefs are but worldly sorrow, I answer, that the question is not what kind of sorrow it is, so much as what the effects of it is. For no matter what the sorrow is, if it drive the soul to Christ, our salvation is by Christ, and not by sorrow. The use of sorrow is to embitter sin, and the world, and to drive the soul to Christ for relief and rest. If worldly sorrow, or rather sorrow about worldly things do this, it hath its end, and proves to be a godly sorrow. Sorrows are not to merit anything from God, but to force the afflicted soul to fly to him for refuge. We shall find examples in scripture, where sorrows about worldly things have effectually driven the soul to fly to God for refuse. Psalm 88:18, Lover and friend hast thou put far from me, and mine acquaintance into darkness. This was an outward affliction, and yet in the first verse of that psalm it drives him to fly and cry to the God of his salvation. And this is an act of faith. So Psalm 35:15, But in mine adversity they rejoiced, and gathered themselves together: yea, the abjects gathered themselves together against me, and I knew it not; they did tear me, and ceased not; that is, some broke jests upon him at their taverns and tipplings, and others scorned him, etc. All these were outward afflictions, but they drove David to fly and cry to God, verse 17, Lord, how long wilt thou look on? rescue my soul from their destructions, my darling from the lions, and this is an act of faith. So it was with Job in his affliction, Job 30:8-10. The basest of the people made songs and jests upon him, but mark what end God made with Job. So James speaks, James 5:12. Therefore whatever your griefs be, turn them into prayers, and cry to God for relief. And then your grief hath a sanctified end, and you will at last learn to say after David, in that high strained string of faith and experience, It is good for me that I have been afflicted; that I might learn thy statutes, Psalm 119:71. And verse 67 of that Psalm, Before I was afflicted I went astray: but now have I kept thy word. And therefore what though your afflictions be outward afflictions, seeing God is pleased mercifully to bless them unto your spiritual and eternal good.

But I further observe, that sundry of your expressions do hold forth a spiritual sorrow for your sin, and a fear of God's wrath, and an earnest desire to flee from, and escape wrath to come. I pray therefore express yourself what sorrows and griefs you have of that kind. For although such sorrows do not deserve anything at God's hand, yet they are of a more spiritual nature, and spring from a deep reverence and fear of God, and do more immediately and effectually drive the soul for refuge to Jesus Christ, who only delivereth the soul from the guilt and condemnation of sin. Utter some drops of those soul-wounding terrors, which afflict you in the sense of your sin guiltiness.

PENIT.   Still my soul admireth to see the great use that is to be made of the Word of God, which doth engage my soul more and more, to the frequent use of the scriptures. Lord Jesus Christ help me to perform it.

My fore-mentioned griefs about my outward condition are but the porch of those troubles that lodge in my distressed soul. When I look down into the dungeon of my heart, and the dunghill of my life, I am filled with an abhorrence of myself, and wonderment of God's patience, to suffer such a wretch as I am to live. I know much of the sins of others, but I know more by my self, than I know of anybody else, considering circumstantial aggravations. I can truly say with Paul, I Timothy 1:15, sinners, of whom I am chief. If my companions have misled me, or my leaders have caused me to err, it may aggravate their sin, but be no excuse or apology for mine. I have done as evil as I could, and had not God hampered me with outward affliction and trouble, it is not to be said by man how vile I should have been. It is sometimes a quieting argument to my heart, to be patient under my outward crosses, because they be mustard

on the world's nipples, to keep me from surfeiting upon the
creature. If I look into the glass of God's law, and behold the
face of my life, and of my soul, as they are there represented,
I am afraid of my self. I abhor my self. I am confounded. God's
sabbaths have I profaned; God's word I have neglected; God's
grace I have despised and resisted. I have broken the whole
law of God. Every command have I violated. For there be some
acts of sin that I never did actually commit, yet the habit of
sin is in me, and in inclination and desire I am guilty of it. And
for a foundation of this mountainous heap of guilt, I am guilty
of Adam's fall, the first, the worst, the root of all the sins of
the sons of men. My sinful habit and disposition by nature
doth viciously incline me to sin against my desires, purposes,
promises, and resolutions. When I strive and labor and cry and
pray against my sins, yet upon the opportunity and occasion
offered, my sin will return. I am weak, that is strong. I am sub-
dued, and that prevaileth. *Oh wretched man that I am, who
shall deliver me?*[50]

When I consider the infinite justice of God offended, the
infinite wrath of God provoked, the eternal law of God violated,
and the eternal torments provided and prepared in hell for
sinners, and the insuperableness of my sin, by any means I can
use, it will prevail over me. It will keep me in bondage, it will
enslave me, and I fear it finally will damn me. In these considerations my soul is sunk and drowned. If therefore there be
any balm for my sore, any succor for my distressed soul, show
me the way how I shall escape these everlasting burnings, that
are the just recompense of my transgressions.

JOHN.   The first endeavor of the heart of man is to pacify God's
wrath with something of our own; and first by mincing, excusing
and apologizing, as they did. Jeremiah 2:33-37, Why trimmest
thou thy way to seek love? Thou searchest ways and acts to
sin cunningly; and hence the blood of innocent souls is openly
found in thy skirts. Yet thou sayest, I am innocent, and his
anger shall be turned away. But then divine Justice taketh the
cause in hand. Why gaddest thou about to seek so many shifts?
I will never leave thee til I have made thee ashamed of them all,

for none of them shall prosper to turn away divine wrath, or
to procure thee a pardon. But I find not your soul mincing of
your sin, nor making excuses for your self.

The next course the heart of man will take is to purchase a
pardon, by giving to God some great sacrifice, or by doing some
great penance. As it is expressed in Micah 6:6-8, Wherewith
shall I come before the Lord, and bow myself before the high
God? shall I come before him with burnt offerings, with calves
of a year old? Will the Lord be pleased with thousands of rams,
or with ten thousands of rivers of oil? Shall I give my firstborn
for my transgression, the fruit of my body for the sin of my
soul? He hath showed thee, O man, what is good; and what
doth the Lord require of thee, but to do justly, and to love
mercy and to walk humbly with thy God? The inquiry is wherewith a sinner shall pacify God. He proffers great matters, more
than he can perform. He bids low at first, only burnt offerings
and calves. But when that will not be accepted, he rises higher,
showing what he would do if he had wherewith. He bids thousands of rams, ten thousand rivers of oil. If that will not do,
he offers the fruit of his body for the sin of his soul, whether
macerations of the body, or any other fruit. But alas, all will
not do. And then, verse 8, he shows what is the only thing
that will satisfy, only Jesus Christ, believed on by faith, held
forth in those works of sanctification and holy life, for so the
scripture testifies, II Corinthians 5:19, To wit, that God was
in Christ, reconciling the world unto himself, not imputing
their trespasses unto them; and hath committed unto us the
word of reconciliation. And Acts 4:12, Neither is there salvation in any other: for there is none other name under heaven
given among men, whereby we must be saved. Acts 16:31,
And they said, Believe on the Lord Jesus Christ, and thou shalt
be saved, and thy house. I do not mention such texts of scripture as calls to repentance, because the end of repentance being
to dispose the heart to believing, it seemeth to me, by your
many and gracious confessions, that the spirit of God hath
wrought in you a penitent heart already, and your soul lieth
in the very next capacity of believing in our Lord Jesus Christ
by the promise. Yea further I say, that your gracious acceptance
of the word of God, love unto it, and submission to its light

and conduct, these acts of grace in you are so powerful, sweet
and savory, that I know not but that the work of faith is already wrought in your poor, mourning, trembling, but blessed
soul. And therefore be no more so disconsolate, hope in the
Lord, and do as it is said, Psalm 27:14, Wait on the Lord, be of
good courage, and he shall strengthen thy heart: wait I say,
upon the Lord.

PENIT. I do perceive that you take that to be a great work of
grace and faith in my heart, so gladly to receive the word of
God, and submissively to give up my self to the conduct thereof.
I cannot deny, but confess, that my heart is really so as I have
expressed, and everything that hath passed in this conference
hath had something in it to strengthen that frame of heart in
me. And now lastly and especially, that you do bring forth that
work which is wrought in me to be an evidence of faith, this
doth so much the more incline and oblige my heart to a great
love and reverence to the scriptures, and a resolution, through
the grace, help and assistance of Jesus Christ, to spend the rest
of my life in a more diligent and abundant attendance on the
hearing, reading, meditating on, and obeying of the Word of
God. If this be an act of faith, I desire to live that part of the
life of faith all the days of my life. Lord help me to perform
this promise unto God.

JOHN. I will show you the reason why I lay so much weight
upon that fear of heart, to embrace the word, to love it, to obey
it, etc. First, I find that it is the character of those famous primi-
tive converts, Acts 2:41-42, Then they that gladly received his
word were baptized: and the same day there were added unto
them about three thousand souls. And they continued stead-
fastly in the apostle's doctrine and fellowship, and in breaking
of bread, and in prayers. Their obedience to, and walking in
the word, is a chief effect and sign of the true and thorough
work of grace in them. In that point their conversion shined,
and it seemeth to me, that your conversion doth in this point
shine.

  Again, James 1:21, Wherefore lay apart all filthiness and
superfluity of naughtiness, and receive with meekness the en-

grafted word, which is able to save your souls. Here be three
things in this text. The first is the preparative work, to cast
away all filthiness, and outboilings of naughtiness. This work
God hath wrought in your distressed heart, which appeareth in
your penitent confessions. The second work is to receive the
word with meekness, and so, that it may appear to be an engrafted word, connaturalized in your heart; which is the work
of faith, whereby you are united to Christ by the word so received, and submitted unto. The entrance of thy words giveth
light; it giveth understanding unto the simple, Psalm 119:130.
Then the third thing. This word so received and engrafted,
whereby you are united to Christ. This will save your soul.
You are a vessel of grace, and shall be a vessel of glory. Fear it   .
not. God that cannot lie hath spoken it.

Again, I Peter 2:1-2, Wherefore laying aside all malice, and
all guile, and hypocrisies, and envies, and all evil speakings,
as newborn babes, desire the sincere milk of the word, that yet
may grow thereby. Here see a newborn babe, that is, a soul converted, a new creature formed in the heart by faith laying hold
on Christ, and from him receiving the spirit, to dwell in him,
and to form this new creature in his heart. Now what acts of
life doth this babe perform? They are two. By mortification
and repentance he purgeth out his sins, and this act of life you
effectually do by your penitent confessions. The second act of
life is, he desires the sincere milk of the word that he may grow
thereby. The new creature is fed by the same means by which
it was begotten. The Word of God is the feed of God to beget
the new creature, I John 3:9, and then the Word of God is milk
to feed and nourish the new creature. Now this is the thing I
observe in you, that as a newborn babe you desire the milk of
the word. And note this word, *sincere milk*. A living babe of
Christ cannot abide human mixtures added to the Word of
God. He loves the pure word, he cannot relish mixtures.

PENIT.   My dearest friend, God hath made you an instrument
in his hand to lay before me unspeakable consolation. And I
cannot deny but I feel it in my heart. I am another man than
I was. I looked upon my self the most miserable of men. I now

am happy being united with Christ. O blessed change! I am in admiration at this. I admire the grace of God to a dead, lost, damned sinner. I am come into a new world. I have other desire than I had, and other purposes. I see things in another frame than I was wont to see them. I must live a new life, and steer a new course.

But in this point my soul desires to begin. I am not mine own. I am the servant of Jesus Christ. He died for me, and by his grace I desire to live unto him. And now I find myself greatly to need counsel how to order my self in my future course. What shall I do for the Lord, who hath done so much for me? My dear friend, your counsel hath been greatly owned and blessed by the Lord for my new life. I desire to have a great respect for your counsel for the ordering of my ways in my new life.

You do partly know that my people, and some chief ones among them, have had but a small measure of respect for me. But I have great reason to overlook it, and bury it, because in his infinite mercy Christ hath turned it about for my better good. My heart telleth me that I must seek the good of my people. How to manage that work wisely is my difficulty, wherein I need your counsel. I would to God that all my people were as I am, and tasted and felt what I have found. But that is not yet so. I desire to bring them to be the Lord's people. How I shall accomplish that is my great difficulty. You know I have been frequently among you praying Indians. And in my heart have adhered to you, and it may be that I have found the less acceptation for it. But I leave that to God. I must do and perform the trust, charge and duty that my Lord Jesus committed to me. My question therefore is, how shall I comport with the present affairs, and state of things? How shall I bring the matter about, to bring about my people to pray to God?

JOHN. It joys my heart to hear these gracious breathings of God's spirit in you. I taste in your discourse evident tokens of a living child of God. I see that my judgement about the spiritual state of your soul was not a product of precipate charity, but an effect of the spirit of right discerning. I will encourage you in your godly purposes with a modest application of some of the angel's words to Gideon. Judges 6:12, 14, And the angel of the Lord appeared unto him, and said unto him, The Lord is with thee, thou mighty man of valor. And the Lord looked upon him, and said, Go in this thy might, and thou shalt save Israel from the hand of the Midianites: have I not sent thee? But for the manner of your proceeding in this matter, my thoughts incline me to propose this way. Be open to own the grace of God bestowed on you, to confess your former known crooked and dark ways, and the change which God by his grace hath wrought in you. At present, let your first motion be to stay a while at Natick. Adjoin yourself to the church, who when they hear of your confession, will joyfully receive you. In due season, request of the church to send some able, pious, and fitting teachers with you, among your people. Prudent counsel may be taken how to prepare and predispose your people for such a motion. I do not doubt but the Governor and Magistrates of the Massachusetts will be easily entreated to interpose in so good a work, which may tend to the bringing in so many people to the service of Jesus Christ.

PENIT. I do well approve and accept of your counsel. It savoreth of discretion and wisdom. In all things God hath guided your lips to drop like the honey comb into my heart. And now I have one request further unto you, that while we are together in this solitary opportunity, we may spend some time in conversing with God in prayer, turn all those things that have passed into prayers, and the future matters also. Let us spread them before the Lord, and beg his guidance and blessing.

JOHN. I do greatly accept this motion, and it is another sign of the truth of the work of God's grace in your heart, because this is the property of the new creature, a newborn babe, that he will cry abba father.

Here we leave them at prayer.

Finis

Annotations

1. The Commissioners of the United Colonies served as an intercolonial defense agency for Massachusetts Bay, Connecticut, Plymouth Plantation, and New Haven. After 1649 the Commissioners were deeply involved in Indian mission activities as administrators of funds from the New England Company. Harry M. Ward, *The United Colonies of New England, 1643-1699.* New York, 1961.
2. Also known as the New England Company, the Society for the Propagation of the Gospel in New England was chartered by Parliament in 1649 and drew its support from Puritan merchants in London. Eliot's extensive dealings with the Company are traced in William Kellaway, *The New England Company, 1649-1776: Missionary Society to the American Indians.* London, 1961; and Alden T. Vaughan, *New England Frontier Puritans and Indians, 1620-1675.* Boston, 1965.
3. Piumbukhou may be Piambow, a ruling elder at the praying town of Hassanamesitt. He may also be Piam Boohan, a ruler at the praying town of Natick. Daniel Gookin, *Historical Collections of the Indians in New England* (1674), pp. 71, 73. Pagination from the edition by Jeffrey H. Fiske.
4. A Nipmuk Indian village located in Windham County, Connecticut. The word in Nipmuk means "between two river branches." John C. Huden, *Indian Place Names of New England.* New York, 1962, p. 137.
5. Established by John Eliot in 1650, Natick was to be the model praying town for a series of convert villages. Natick was designed as an English village with a meetinghouse, a fort, and streets. *See* John Eliot and Thomas Mayhew, Jr. *Tears of Repentance: Or, A Further Narrative of the Progress of the Gospel amongst the Indians in New England* (1653). Reprinted in Massachusetts Historical Society *Collections*, 3rd. Ser. 4 (1834): 227; Gookin, *Historical Collections*, pp. 65-71; Neal Salisbury, "Red Puritans: The 'Praying Indians' of

Massachusetts Bay and John Eliot." *William and Mary Quarterly*, 3rd Ser. 21 (January 1974): 32-34.

6. Proverbs 10:4.
7. Luke 12:31; Matthew 6:33.
8. A reference to Eliot's Algonkian Indian Bible, first published in 1663.
9. frightening.
10. An allusion to Hebrews 13:9.
11. Piumbukhou was correct in his assessment of the problems English farmers experienced in southern New England. His comment on "blasted corn" is probably a reference to the persistent wheat smut or rust. The Indian had an equally acute eye for urban dangers. Boston houses had highly inflammable roofs and citizens were repeatedly warned about the fire danger.
12. Taubot—I am glad. Roger Williams, *A Key into the Language of America*. Edited by John J. Teunissen and Evelyn J. Hinz. Detroit, 1973, p. 94.
13. Deuteronomy 6:11b-12a.
14. Ephesians 5:14.
15. protection.
16. The ancient name for Martha's Vineyard. Huden, *Indian Place Names*, p. 150.
17. Nantucket.
18. An Indian name for Eastern Long Island. William W. Tooker. *The Indian Names on Long Island*. New York, 1911, p. 182.
19. Mashpee.
20. Eliot gained most of his converts from among the Massachuset, a tribe weakened by disease and the loss of political autonomy.
21. Native peoples of many bands living in the Massachusetts interior east of the Connecticut River were usually called the Nipmuk. In the early 1670s Eliot mounted a major missionary assault on the Nipmuk, establishing eight mission towns and gaining a substantial number of converts. Salisbury, "Red Puritans," pp. 35-36.
22. A southern New England word for leader or headman. Williams, *Key*, p. 201.
23. A southern New England term for priest or healer as well as the act of healing.
24. Deuteronomy 8:3; Matthew 4:4.
25. A southern New England word for master, commander, or ruler. Huden, *Indian Place Names*, p. 326.
26. The medical commentary reflects Eliot's desire to undercut the religious and healing influence of the powwows. James P. Ronda. " 'We

Are Well As We Are': An Indian Critique of Seventeenth-Century Christian Missions." *William and Mary Quarterly*, 3rd Ser. 34 (January 1977):73-74.

27. The Sabbath observance references throughout this section are taken from Exodus 20 and further reflect the codes of conduct drafted for the praying towns.

28. The catechism referred to is Eliot's *The Indian Primer*, first published in 1669. The Algonkian text contained "The Large Catechism" as well as short biblical extracts. James P. Ronda. "The Bible and Early American Indian Missions." In E. Sandeen, ed., *The Bible and Social Reform*. New York, 1980, chapter I.

29. Psalms 106:1; 107:1; 118:1; 136:1.

30. When Eliot began his missionary work among the Massachuset in 1646, one of his first converts was Waban. Although not a sachem, Waban was made "chief minister of Justice" in his village and rigorously enforced English law. Francis Jennings. *The Invasion of America: Indians, Colonialism, and the Cant of Conquest*. Chapel Hill, 1975, pp. 239-42.

31. Peneovot is evidently a character of Eliot's own invention.

32. A Nipmuk sachem whose 1652 confession of faith is recorded in Eliot and Mayhew, *Tears of Repentance*, pp. 249-52.

33. Proverbs 28:14.

34. Genesis 3:19.

35. Psalms 2:9.

36. Psalms 2:10.

37. An Indian preacher at the praying town of Natick, 1669-1675. Frederick L. Weis. "The New England Company of 1649 and Its Missionary Enterprises." *Publications* of the Colonial Society of Massachusetts 38 (1947-1951):181.

38. William Abahton (or Ahaton) was one of Eliot's most promising converts. William was the son of Ahauton, chief ruler of the praying town of Ponkipog. Eliot described William Abahton as "a promising young man, of a single and upright heart, a good judgement, he prayeth and preacheth well. He is studious and industrious, and well accounted of among the English." Abahton saw service with English forces during King Philip's War and acted as preacher at Ponkipog from 1674 to 1717. John Eliot. *A Brief Narrative of the Progresse of the Gospel amongst the Indians in New England*. London, 1671, p. 5; Daniel Gookin. "An Historical Account of the Doings and Sufferings of the Christian Indians of New England in the Years 1675, 1676, and 1677." *Transactions and Collections of the American Antiquarian*

Society 2 (1836):472; Weis, "New England Company," p. 157.

39. Pokanoket, located in Bristol County, Massachusetts. It is a Wampanoag word meaning "at the cleared land" or "fort" or "refuge." Also known as Sowams, it was the home village and favorite place of the Wampanoag sachem Philip. Huden, *Indian Place Names*, p. 191.

40. This is the only known reference to the Wampanoag sachem Metacom as Philip Keitasscot.

41. John Eliot, Junior, eldest son of John Eliot, died in 1668. He was a regular preacher at Ponkipog.

42. Cutshamoquin or Cutshamekin was a principal sachem of the Massachuset Indians. He chose to ally with the Bay colony, fearing assaults from northern tribes as well as the growing stream of English settlers. His power steadily undercut, the sachem finally ended his resistance to conversion and became the first ruler of the new praying town of Natick. Salisbury, "Red Puritans," pp. 35-36.

43. Chikautabuk, also known as Josias or Josiah, became Massachuset ruler at Natick upon the death of Cutshamoquin. Daniel Gookin, writing in 1674, offered the following comments on Chikautabuk and the tensions between the ruler and many converts alluded to by Eliot later in the *Dialogues*. "He had considerable knowledge in the Christian religion and sometime, when he was younger, seemed to profess it for a time—and was a catechised Indian, and kept the Sabbath several years; but after turned apostate, and for several years last past, separated from the praying Indians, and was but a back friend to religion." Gookin, *Historical Collections*, pp. 40-41.

44. Successor to Chikautabuk and third Massachuset ruler at Natick.

45. Onsamequin, also known as Massasoit, was a Wampanoag sachem from about 1620 until his death in 1663.

46. A medical concoction prepared to alleviate pain.

47. At this point there is a break in text pagination. George Parker Winship notes that "the signatures run correctly from A to K_4, but there is a break in the pagination, the numbers 61 to 66 being omitted, so that the customary explanation of work assigned to two compositors working at the same time is unlikely." George Parker Winship. *The Cambridge Press 1638-1692*. Philadelphia, 1945, pp. 321-22.

48. John Speen, described by Daniel Gookin as "grave and pious," was one of the Indian preachers at Natick from 1669 to 1675. His 1652 confession of faith was recorded by Eliot in *Tears of Repentance*, pp. 246-47. *See also* Gookin, *Historical Collections*, p. 71; Weis, "New England Company," p. 181.

49. A paraphrase of Malachi 2:7.

50. Romans 7:24.

Bibliography

Bailey, Alfred G. *The Conflict of European and Eastern Algonkian Cultures, 1504-1700: A Study in Canadian Civilization.* Toronto, 1969.

Bercovitch, Sacvan. *The Puritan Origins of the American Self.* New Haven, 1975.

Breen, Timothy. *The Character of the Good Ruler: Puritan Political Ideas in New England, 1630-1730.* New York, 1970.

Carroll, Peter N. *Puritanism and the Wilderness: The Intellectual Significance of the New England Frontier, 1629-1700.* New York, 1969.

Cook, Sherburne. *The Indian Population of New England in the Seventeenth Century.* Berkeley, 1976.

Eames, Wilberforce, ed. *John Eliot and the Indians, 1652-1657: Being Letters Addressed to Rev. Jonathan Hanmer of Barnstaple, England.* New York, 1915.

Eliot, John. *A Brief Narrative of the Progress of the Gospel Among the Indians of New England.* Cambridge, Mass., 1670.

——. *The Indian Primer.* Cambridge, Mass., 1669.

——, and Mayhew, Thomas Jr. *Tears of Repentance: Or, A Further Narrative of the Progress of the Gospel Amongst the Indians in New England.* London, 1653.

Flannery, Regina. *An Analysis of Coastal Algonquian Culture.* Washington, D.C., 1939.

Gookin, Daniel. *An Historical Account of the Doings and Sufferings of the Christian Indians in New England.* London, 1677.

——. *Historical Collections of the Indians in New England.* Boston, 1792.

Huden, John C. *Indian Place Names of New England.* New York, 1962.

Jacobs, Wilbur R. *Dispossessing the American Indian: Indians and Whites on the Colonial Frontier.* New York, 1972.

Jennings, Francis. *The Invasion of America: Indians, Colonialism, and the Cant of Conquest.* Chapel Hill, 1976.

Kellaway, William. *The New England Company, 1649-1776, Missionary Society to the American Indians.* London, 1961.

Leach, Douglas E. *Flintlock and Tomahawk: New England in King Philip's War.* New York, 1958.

———. *The Northern Colonial Frontier, 1607-1763.* New York, 1966.

Mather, Cotton. *Magnalia Christi Americana; or, The Ecclesiastical History of New England; from its First Planting, in the Year 1620, Unto the Year of Our Lord 1698.* Hartford, 1855.

Morgan, Edmund S. *The Puritan Family: Religion and Domestic Relations in Seventeenth-Century New England.* Boston, 1944.

Peckham, Howard, and Gibson, Charles, eds. *Attitudes of Colonial Powers Toward the American Indian.* Salt Lake City, 1969.

Ronda, James P. "The Bible and Early American Indian Missions." In Ernest Sandeen, ed. *The Bible and Social Reform.* New York, 1980.

———. " 'We Are Well as We Are': An Indian Critique of Seventeenth Century Christian Missions." *William and Mary Quarterly* 3rd ser., 34 (January 1977): 66-82.

Salisbury, Neal. "Red Puritans: The 'Praying Indians' of Massachusetts Bay and John Eliot." *William and Mary Quarterly* 3rd ser., 31 (January 1974): 27-54.

Shuffleton, Frank. "Indian Devils and Pilgrim Fathers: Squanto, Hobomok, and the English Conception of Indian Religion." *New England Quarterly* 44 (March 1976): 108-16.

Simmons, William S. *Cautantowwit's House: An Indian Burial Ground on the Island of Conanicut in Narragansett Bay.* Providence, 1970.

———. "Southern New England Shamanism: An Ethnographic Reconstruction." In William Cowan, ed. *Papers of the Seventh Algonkian Conference.* Ottawa, 1975, pp. 217-56.

———. "Conversion from Indian to Puritan." *New England Quarterly* 52 (June 1979): 197-218.

Slotkin, Richard. *Regeneration through Violence: The Mythology of the American Frontier, 1600-1800.* Middletown, 1973.

Smith, James M., ed. *Seventeenth-Century America: Essays in Colonial History.* Chapel Hill, 1959.

Vaughan, Alden T. *The New England Frontier: Puritans and Indians, 1620-1675.* Boston, 1965.

Walker, Williston. *Ten New England Leaders.* New York, 1901.

Ward, Harry M. *The United Colonies of New England, 1643-1690.* New York, 1961.

Weis, Frederick L. "The New England Company of 1649 and Its Mission-
    ary Enterprises." Colonial Society of Massachusetts, *Transactions* 38
    (1947-1951).
Williams, Roger. *A Key into the Language of America.* London, 1643.
Winship, George P. *The Cambridge Press, 1638-1692.* Philadelphia, 1945.
Winslow, Ola E. *John Eliot, "Apostle to the Indians."* Boston, 1968.
Wroth, Lawrence C. *The Colonial Printer.* New York, 1938.

Index

About the Authors

HENRY W. BOWDEN is Professor of Religion at Douglass College in New Brunswick, New Jersey. He is the author of *Church History in the Age of Science* and *Dictionary of American Religious Biography* (Greenwood Press, 1977).

JAMES P. RONDA is Professor of History at Youngstown State University in Youngstown, Ohio. His earlier works include *Indian Missions: A Critical Bibliography* and *A Teacher's Guide to the American Revolution.*